PORSCHE 911

with Targa, Carrera, Convertible
1963—86

PORSCHE 911

with Targa, Carrera, Convertible

1963-86

A Documentation by Walter Zeichner

1469 Morstein Road, West Chester, Pennsylvania 19380

One need not waste many words about the significance of the Porsche 911 as a milestone on the international sports car scene. But it is very interesting to trace the long life history of this legendary automobile from Stuttgart through its advertisements—and that is the contents of this book. The row of models runs from the first 901 to the last catalyzer Carrera, and in terms of the available space, only a few good examples from the usually superbly prepared catalogs and brochures can be shown. Thanks for their support in this project go to the publicity department of the Dr. Ing. h. c. F. Porsche AG, as well as to Georg Amtmann, Kai Jacobsen and Robert Horender, who have provided the exhaustive list of all miniature models.

Halwart Schrader
Editor

Contents

Porsche 911—a Legend

There are few automobiles that are allowed to keep their basic external form for more than 25 years and whose basic technical concepts have remained the same over this long period of time, save for numerous improvements and further developments. One of these cars that are "classics in their own time" doubtless is the Porsche 911, which even today has lost none of its popularity. Drivers of the 911 form a loyal community to whom their car means far more than a driveable seat. Driving a 911 means being part of a sports car philosophy that makes one immune to the ever-so-alluring offerings of other manufacturers. Yet the 911 was never the fastest, costliest or prettiest sports car that was or still is on the market; comparable English cars have offered more exclusive equipment, and Italian cars more frequently have drawn attention to themselves with their often breathtaking bodies. What is this phenomenon, the Porsche 911?

It would be excessive to go deeply into the closely related histories of the firm and the Porsche family here. It began with the 356 mythos, still closely related to the Volkswagen Beetle. But since about 1956 plans were made for a successor to this car. The bodywork should conform more to modern taste, with larger windows and stricter lines, but one should be able to tell at first glance that the car came from Zuffenhausen. Thus the new car's similarity to the 356, which was built parallel to it until 1965, is unmistakable, above all in the characteristic fastback and the front end. Ferdinand "Butzi" Porsche, a grandson of the firm's founder, also had experimented with the design of a stepback car, in which the rear-seat passengers had considerably more room, but the firm turned away from this idea and stayed with the traditional 2+Œ2 style. As a power plant for the sports car, which was first called the 901, a six-cylinder air-cooled boxer motor was chosen, one with which the firm had had good experiences for years, and the rear engine position was also retained, since this promised to be the most advantageous solution for later racing use.

The heat problems that are inherent in such a motor caused the Porsche technicians no problems, and there also was confidence about the sound damping of the air-cooled sports motor. But there was particular concern about finding considerably more usable space than in the 356. The Porsche 901 was to be not only a sporting vehicle, but also above all a fast touring car with the ability to carry normal luggage. The greatest plus in storage space was under the car's front hood, since the spare tire and fuel tank were mounted low and the steering drive was installed close to the bottom. The new space-saving front wheel suspension, with transverse links and MacPherson struts, also contributed much to this gain in space, which along with longitudinal links and torsion bars on the rear axle contributed to pleasant, not-too-hard-yet-sufficiently-stiff suspension characteristics. The new six-cylinder light metal motor was planned from the start to have considerable possibilities for development. With a stroke-to-bore ratio of 66 to 80 mm, it very definitely was a short-stroke motor, characterized even at its highest speeds by comparatively low piston speeds that contributed to long engine life. The crankshaft had eight bearings and each of the two cylinder blocks had a chain-driven camshaft. Also noteworthy was the dry-sump lubrication, suitable for a racing car, that could supply the machine with oil even under the highest stress and also contribute to cooling the crankcase.

With a compression ratio of 9:1, this splendidly constructed motor produced 130 hp at a speed of 6200

Left: Rear view of the new 911, which was still known as the 901 when introduced, as this photo shows.

Below: The 901, alias 911 prototype of 1963, as shown at the Frankfurt International Auto Show.

rpm, which the light and precise five-speed Porsche gearbox translated into just over 125 mph. Effective disc brakes on all four wheels took care of safe reduction of such high speed, and one felt quite comfortable in the neatly designed interior, with its upright seats and clear arrangement of the instruments and controls. The tachometer, as in many sports cars, was the most important and largest gauge, and was situated in the middle between the combined gauge and speedometer, right in front of the driver on the dashboard, which was padded above and below. The steering wheel had four spokes. If the workmanship was less than perfect at the beginning, this soon changed, and the car satisfied its owners fully in this area too; everything seemed to have been cast in one and the same mold. The type number led to unexpected difficulties when the car was shown at the 1963 Frankfurt Automobile Show, where the Peugeot firm soon pointed out that three-digit numbers with a zero in the middle traditionally were reserved for their cars. Porsche did not want to have any difficulties with sales of their new sports car in France, so from then on the most successful Porsche of all time was called 911.

When production of the 911 began at the end of 1964, the price was set at 21,900 Marks, a sum that many loyal Porsche drivers could not afford. The price would have forced them to change to other brands if Porsche had not anticipated this. In April of 1965 Porsche presented the four-cylinder 912 model in the same body as the 911; it had the slightly detuned 90-hp motor of the old 1600-SC model in its rear and cost only 16,000 Marks. Thus many former 356 drivers could afford a new Porsche that could scarcely be told from the 911 externally and also offered noteworthy performance, with a top speed of 115 mph. Though the first 150 examples of this

7

Front, rear and three-quarter views of the 2-liter Porsche 911 S of 1964 in its lightweight version.

reasonably priced sports cars still had painted sheet metal dashboards, this soon changed, and after that the 912 could scarcely be told apart from the 911. The 912 was built without essential changes until 1968, and thanks to its lower price it found more customers than even the 911, which was much in demand. In 1975 there was a new 912 version in the form of the 912 E, which was made exclusively for the overseas market and had the motor of the 914-4.

A year after production of the 911/912 began, Porsche presented another sensation in September of 1965: the Targa. This car was the first safety convertible in the world, for a massive, wide roll bar assured that driving an open car no longer involved as much risk as before, when turning an open car over often resulted in fatalities. This body type offered many possible variations, but because of the wide roll bar, one did not have the same feeling as in a true convertible. Yet many customers chose this variation, which was available with all engine types.

In November of 1966 there was good news for achievement-minded Porsche drivers. A new, more powerful model—the 911 S—was announced for the coming year. With a changed cylinder head, forged pistons, slightly nitrated connecting rods, a more

precise camshaft, and bigger air vents, the motor now easily turned out 160 hp at 6600 rpm and made possible a top speed of 140 mph. Internally cooled disc brakes and Koni shock absorbers complemented the improvement, which also included such interior details as a leather-covered steering wheel and better carpeting. The warning area of the tachometer now began at 7300 rpm, and if the motor was driven too fast, a governor was engaged to prevent damage to the motor.

The normal 911 now was called 911 L (Luxury), and as of August 1967 there was a further version, the 911 T (Touring), with 110 hp, for sport drivers with a little less concern for performance. Whoever paid an additional 990 Marks received a semi-automatic four-speed transmission called "Sportomatic," which eliminated the clutch. This especially was important for the American market, where cars with standard transmissions almost were impossible to sell.

Despite the detuned motor, the 911 T was no lame duck, but accelerated from zero to 62 mph in 10.5 seconds, only one second slower than the 911 L with its 130 hp. Only the 130-hp 911 S clearly showed its superiority in this respect with a time of barely eight seconds. In 1968 too the 911 L and 911 S were given mechanical fuel injection in place of the somewhat problematic Weber carburetor, which made both motors some ten hp more powerful. The L-model was called 911 E henceforth.

In the very next year all models were given a new performance boost, as the motors were bored out by 4 mm and now displaced 2.2 liters. Even the "weakest" Porsche 911 T (production of the 912 ended in 1968) now had 125 hp and easily exceeded 125 mph. The fuel-injected types now offered 155 and 180 hp, and the 911 S in particular profited from the increased bore in terms of clearly improved flexibility. The interiors of the new models also were nicely improved, but the functional atmosphere was kept, and a particular plus from now on was the zinc plating of parts, which contributed much to preserving the car's value.

As of 1971 a new generation of motors began their work under the Porsche 911's rear hood. As a reaction to the more stringent pollution regulations in the USA, the motors were adapted to run on normal gasoline and, with their stroke lengthened by 4.4 mm, reached a displacement of 2.4 liters, which meant newly increased performance for all three 911 types. But constantly increasing top speeds caused ever-higher demands on the 911's driving stability,

and so the 911 S, now at 190 hp and reaching about 149 mph, was given a front spoiler, which soon went into series production for the E and T models too. Improved weight distribution and wider tires also did their share. With steadily improved performance, a new gearbox was needed, with first and second gears in one plane. A four-speed version was made standard, with five speeds optional. The car also could be had with an optional 22.25-gallon fuel tank, which was combined with a new-type collapsible spare tire that could be inflated from a compressed-air tank so as not to take away too much of the luggage space. In 1973 the recently introduced oil filler of the 2.4-liter models, located under the righthand pillar, was eliminated, having caused much damage by being confused with the fuel filler. Unfortunately, the versions of the 911 that ran on normal fuel burned considerably more of it than before, but could anyone who could afford a not-exactly cheap Porsche complain about that? On the other hand, the 911 models now had reached a very high standard in terms of maturity, quality of workmanship and reliability, which promised an excellent resale value for the price.

To keep up with the grand touring cars in auto racing, the now legendary "Carrera RS" appeared in 1972, with its 911-S engine bored out to 2.7 liters and producing 210 hp. The top 356 models had become famous as Carreras, named after the Carrera Panamericana, a long-distance auto race in Mexico, in which Porsche cars had had great success. For a price of only 33,000 Marks (Porsche had to sell 500 examples as fast as possible to attain sanction in the GT category) one bought a really impressive car with, if one wanted, race-worthy Spartan furnishings. All the details that were regarded as inessential for racing were missing from the RS Sport, such as back seats, door linings, armrests and storage boxes; even sound-damping material was dispensed with, something not to be omitted in the motor trade. A pure racing atmosphere prevailed in this coupe. Wide tires made widened fenders necessary, which looked very good on the car, and a polyester rear spoiler gave the car its characteristic appearance, along with the spirited Carrera lettering in red, blue or green along the bottom of the doors. Many owners of "normal" 911's now screwed spoilers onto the tails so they could drive around with the Carrera look, but the difference was noted only at top speed if at all. The Carrera driver needed barely six seconds to reach 62 mph, and the light sport version even was a bit faster.

In the fall of 1973, the other 911 models were given the 2.7-liter motor, and a new-type nomenclature was introduced. In practice, the 911 T no longer existed; the least powerful 911 was now the 150-hp 911 without an additional letter. The 911 S now had 175 hp and the Carrera, thanks to great demand, likewise was included in normal series production, with the light version being dropped. The 911 and 911 S now had Bosch-K-Jetronic fuel injection, and the Carrera's old rear spoiler disappeared along with the striking lettering. A new special option, a new flat rear spoiler with rubber rim, was mounted. The bumpers of the new 2.7-liter models also differed essentially from their predecessors by having shock absorbers with folded air chambers, which went very well with the form of the car. Inside the car one first noticed racing seats with integral headrests and extended safety padding for all operational controls. The Carrera received standard electric window lifters.

Above: A 1972 2.7-liter Porsche Carrera with the typical rear spoiler; under it a 1973 Targa.

A 2.4-liter 911 of 1972 vintage.

The end came for the 911 S in 1976. The basic model was now the 911 with 165-hp motor; one also could have automatic speed regulation, known as "Tempostat," built in to hold a steady speed independently once it had been attained without requiring that the driver continue to give gas. The Carrera models, whose appearance won them a very extraordinary position among international sports cars, already were regarded as particularly desirable collector cars.

But even after the Carrera was introduced, the subject of performance was not exhausted at Porsche, for the presentation of the 930 Turbo at Paris in 1974 could be said to mark the dawn of a new era. Though until then there still were English and Italian high-performance sports cars that a Carrera could not equal, suddenly in the mid-seventies the matter was quickly cleared up. The turbocharged engine's announced power of 260 hp at 5500 rpm was no exaggeration of the actual, literally breathtaking performance of this car. Though the unsupercharged power plant with its compression ratio of only 6.5:1 for everyday driving might remind one of a tuned

VW motor, the situation changed very suddenly and dramatically as soon as the driver pushed the gas pedal down all the way and the turbocharger built up 0.8 atmospheres of pressure. The experience of feeling that acceleration often was compared to a kick in the small of the driver's back, and this was not a bad comparison. There probably was no production sports car in the world that made its power felt in a comparably brutal way as the Porsche Turbo, which even had its engine displacement increased to 3.3 liters in 1978. This produced about 300 hp with its turbo-driven air cooler, with the engine now reaching the limit of its developmental potential.

Many construction details of competition cars were utilized in Porsche's top turbo model. Major modifications in chassis, bodywork and power train were necessary to make this extremely fast car safely manageable. This great technical distance from the usual Porsche 911 sports car also is seen in its nonsequential 930 number.

In 1975 the Carrera again was evaluated optically and technically and presented in the form of the Carrera 3.0 model, which provided its 200 hp in a more cultivated and relaxed manner than its predecessor with its 2.7-liter displacement and nervous nature. Luxurious additions such as electrically adjusted and heated side mirrors, automatic heat regulation, and a headlight washing system also lived up to international standards of equipment. Matt black chrome parts and wide fenders symbolized sportiness externally.

Three years later came the end of the 911 and the Carrera, which seemingly merged in the 911 SC that was given the Carrera motor detuned to 180 hp, could run on normal gasoline and was good for 143 mph. The car had electronic ignition, an electronic rpm indicator, and in the long list of extras there appeared the rear spoiler of the 930 Turbo. The motor of this very highly refined car was the model of flexibility; one could drive the car without shifting frequently, as it could go under 25 mph in fifth gear without making the engine stutter. The engine's tremendous moment of inertia even was increased in 1980, when the compression was raised from 8.5:1 to 9.8:1, after which the 911 SC was to be run on premium fuel. The 911 SC reached its high point of 204 hp, which added a bit to the three-liter car's top speed, but beyond that the model could not be improved. Even the "cheapest" Porsche 911 now ran easily at 143 mph.

In 1984 the Carrera celebrated its reincarnation to fill the hole between the SC and the Turbo. For this purpose the 3-liter SC motor had its stroke lengthened by using the Turbo's crankshaft to give a displacement of 3164 cc. The bore remained the same at 94 mm. At the same time the compression was raised to 10.3:1, delivering 231 hp to the clutch, with which the present-day Carrera reaches almost 155 mph.

But back to 1982, when the dreams of many Porsche fans came true with the Porsche 911 full convertible. Since the days of the 356-C convertible they had longed for a completely open Porsche, and the Targa had not been seen as a complete substitute. This new convertible looks good from every angle, and the manually operated top shows its practicality in its thickness and simplicity. It harmonizes perfectly with the body lines and inflates so little, even at high speed, that the same top speeds can be attained with it as with the coupe. Only minor

Left: Porsche 911 R, 1972 model.

Above: 911 SC 3 liter
and 911 Turbo 3.3 liter
of 1980. At left a 911 S
Targa of the 1976-77
generation.

stiffening had to be added to the body, and thus the convertible is not heavier than the hardtop type, an outstanding indication of its quality. Riding in this dream car enhances the enjoyment of driving, which the normal 911 already offers in abundance. One hears, smells and feels more keenly what is in the car and its surroundings, and experiences Porsche driving more intensely.

In 1987 the Carrera was available as a coupe, Targa or convertible, and the Turbo as a coupe or as a convertible. The Porsche 911 has used its long period of development to become the ideal sports car, and it will remain so until the demand for this classis car drops significantly. But if it is sustained, when should production ever end?

It Began with the 901

When interested Porsche fans were given the first brochures of the "new Porsche" at the 1963 Auto Show, they received the folded page shown here. The car shown and described there in not very dramatic

The firm of Dr.-Ing. F. Porsche has created in the Type 901 economical and fast car that, in accordance with the typical Porsche line, unites in itself all the advantages of the proved 356 models and long years of experience of its constructors and test engineers rounds off the current sales program at the top. Equivalent to Carrera 2000 GS in weight and temperament, far exceeding it in te of top speed, the Type 901 will prove anew the old Porsche form "Driving in its most beautiful form". This model provides optimum of riding comfort, roadholding and driving safety, such the discerning Porsche customer had been accustomed to since appearance of the first Porsche car.

The motor is an air-cooled six-cylinder boxer type with sir overhead camshaft on each bank, its construction enriched by experience of Grand Prix and sports car motor development. crankshaft has eight bearings. Light metal is used extensively in motor's components. In terms of construction, the motor is desig so that it can be used for sporting purposes within the parameters o developmental stages. The two camshafts are chain-driven for the ti time in Porsche history. A new gearbox was developed for the equaling the previous one in all its functions but providing forward gears on account of the great range of speed. The fr suspension and handling are provided for by lower transverse l and two shock absorbers, the springing by longitudinal torsion b Rear-wheel suspension and handling are controlled by longitud links supported by transverse torsion bars. The driving powe transmitted by two half-shafts.

The steering operates on the rack-and-pinion principle an located in front, in the center of the car. This means of construc has made possible a significant contribution to interior safety, as use of a stiff steering column could be avoided by rerouting. The ca equipped with disc brakes on all four wheels.

For the bodywork it was necessary to combine the new aggreg into a unity and create greater interior space within the exte dimensions, which exceed those of the Type 356 by only 120 mm length, while a decrease of 70 mm in width has been achieved. At same time, larger window areas were created, in accordance v present-day requirements.

The front seat space could be expanded in terms of the inte dimensions despite the decreased width of the vehicle. The present position, which offers ample comfort on long trips, was maintaine principle. The foot space behind the front seats was expande approximately six centimeters. To make repair work easier, the fr fenders can be removed. In order to comply with present-requirements for the ventilation of the passenger compartm particular attention has been paid to the solution of this matter. Ur the front hood there is abundant space for the storage of suitcases other pieces of luggage.

Above: Title page of the 1963 Porsche brochure for the six-cylinder car then called the 901. This brochure, not very dramatic in its dramatic in its graphics, is highly valued by fans today because it no longer was used after the 1963 Auto Show.

Right: Detailed description of the 901 alias 911. Factual and dispassionate, but giving all the technical details. The luggage space actually was very much bigger than that of the 356 (which continued to be built for a time).

Die Dr.-Ing. h. c. F. Porsche KG. hat mit dem Typ 901 ein wirtschaftliches und schnelles Automobil geschaffen, das unter Berücksichtigung der typischen Porsche-Linie alle Vorzüge der bewährten 356-Modelle und die langjährigen Erfahrungen seiner Konstrukteure und Versuchsingenieure in sich vereint. Es rundet das gegenwärtige Verkaufs-Programm nach oben ab. Im Gewicht und Temperament dem Carrera 2000 GS ebenbürtig, in den Endgeschwindigkeitswerten ihn noch übertreffend, wird der Typ 901 die alte Porsche-Formel „Fahren in seiner schönsten Form" von neuem beweisen. Dieses Modell stellt ein Optimum an Fahrkomfort, Straßenlage und Fahrsicherheit dar, wie es der anspruchsvolle Porsche-Kunde seit Erscheinen des ersten Porsche-Wagens gewöhnt war.

Der Motor ist ein luftgekühlter 6-Zylinder-Boxer-Motor mit je einer obenliegenden Nockenwelle, bei dessen Konstruktion die Erfahrungen der Grand-Prix- und Sportmotorenentwicklung verwertet wurden. Die Kurbelwelle ist achtfach gelagert. Für die Bauteile wurde weitgehend Leichtmetall verwendet. Konstruktiv ist der Motor so

style carried the type number 901. Of course the car could not yet be bought—one had to be patient until the end of 1964. When the first cars of the new six-cylinder production run were delivered, they were no longer called 901 but 911. Which disturbed nobody. A Porsche of those days now has become an "old timer," a valuable classic with the status of a collector's item.

ausgelegt, daß er im Rahmen seiner Entwicklungsstufen für Sportzwecke verwendet werden kann. Die beiden Nockenwellen werden, erstmals bei Porsche, über Ketten angetrieben. Für das Fahrzeug wurde ein neues Getriebe entwickelt, welches in seiner Funktion dem bisherigen gleicht, jedoch wegen des großen Geschwindigkeitsbereiches 5 Vorwärtsgänge besitzt. Die vordere Radaufhängung und Führung erfolgt durch untenliegende Querlenker und die beiden Stoßdämpfer, die Abfederung durch längsliegende Torsionsstäbe. Aufhängung und Führung der Hinterräder werden von Längslenkern übernommen, die über querliegende Drehstäbe abgestützt sind. Der Antrieb erfolgt über Doppelgelenkwellen.

Die Lenkung arbeitet nach dem Zahnstangenprinzip und wurde vorn in der Fahrzeugmitte angeordnet. Diese Bauweise ermöglichte es, einen wesentlichen Beitrag zur inneren Sicherheit zu leisten, da durch den Einbau der Umlenkungen die Verwendung einer starren Lenksäule vermieden werden konnte. Das Fahrzeug ist an allen vier Rädern mit Scheibenbremsen ausgestattet.

Für die Karosserie ergab sich nun die Notwendigkeit, die neuen Aggregate zu einer Einheit zusammenzufassen und bei den äußeren Abmessungen, die den Typ 356 lediglich in der Länge um 120 mm übertreffen, während in der Breite eine Einsparung von 70 mm erzielt werden konnte, einen größeren Innenraum zu schaffen. Gleichzeitig wurden, den heutigen Forderungen entsprechend, größere Fensterflächen geschaffen.

Der Vordersitzraum konnte in den Innenabmessungen trotz geringerer Fahrzeugbreite vergrößert werden. Im Prinzip wurde die heutige Sitzposition, die guten Komfort bei langen Reisen bietet, übernommen. Der Fußraum hinter den Vordersitzen wurde um etwa 6 cm verlängert. Zur Erleichterung bei Instandsetzungsarbeiten können die vorderen Kotflügel ausgewechselt werden. Um bei der Belüftung des Fahrgastraumes den heutigen Ansprüchen gerecht zu werden, wurde der Lösung dieser Frage besondere Aufmerksamkeit geschenkt. Unter der Vorderhaube ist reichlich Raum für die Unterbringung von Koffern und sonstigen Gepäckstücken.

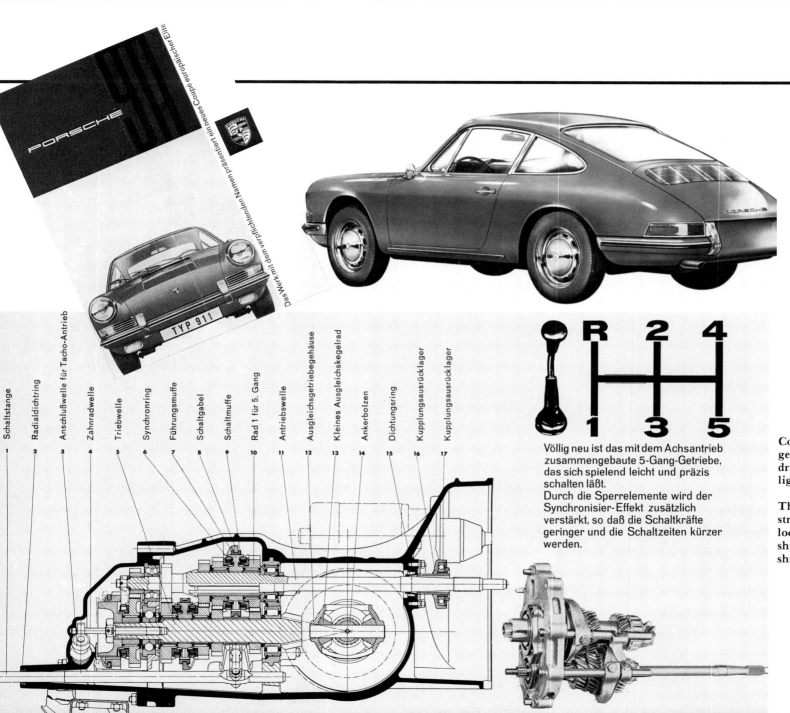

TYP 911

PORSCHE

The factory with the reputation for conscientiousness presents a new European elite coupe.

Numbered items

1 Shift rod

2 Radial seal ring

3 Tachometer drive rod

4 Gear shaft

5 Drive shaft

6 Synchro ring

7 Drive coupling

8 Shift fork

9 Shift coupling

10 Fifth gear

11 Power shaft

12 Equalizing drive housing

13 Small equalizing wheel

14 Anchor bolt

15 Reinforcing ring

16 Clutch bearing

17 Clutch bearing

1	2	3	4	5	6	7	8	9	10	11	12	13	14	15	16	17
Schaltstange	Radialdichtring	Anschlußwelle für Tacho-Antrieb	Zahnradwelle	Triebwelle	Synchronring	Führungsmuffe	Schaltgabel	Schaltmuffe	Rad 1 für 5. Gang	Antriebswelle	Ausgleichsgetriebegehäuse	Kleines Ausgleichskegelrad	Ankerbolzen	Dichtungsring	Kupplungsausrücklager	Kupplungsausrücklager

Völlig neu ist das mit dem Achsantrieb zusammengebaute 5-Gang-Getriebe, das sich spielend leicht und präzis schalten läßt.
Durch die Sperrelemente wird der Synchronisier-Effekt zusätzlich verstärkt, so daß die Schaltkräfte geringer und die Schaltzeiten kürzer werden.

Completely new is the 5-speed gearbox built integrally with the drive axle, which allows playfully light and precise shifting.

The synchronizing effect is strengthened additionally by the locking elements, so that the shifting power becomes less and shifting time becomes shorter.

workmanship with quality materials, almost on a hand-
basis, as well as driver safety as the highest construction
ple, characterize the Porsche 911 too, whose body, thanks to
w beltline, has large windows which allow an almost
ted panoramic view. Wide-opening doors that lock in
make getting in or out from front or back easier. In the
nically designed seats one feels before the car moves the
ance, particularly in fast cars, of the often-absent feeling of
held in the seat. Just as the percentage of usable space for
and passengers represents the highest amount in the GT
he same is true of the oversize luggage space under the front

Solide Verarbeitung gediegener Materialien auf beinahe handwerklicher
Basis sowie Fahrsicherheit als oberstes Konstruktionsprinzip kennzeich-
nen auch den Porsche 911, dessen Karosserie dank der tiefgelegten
Gürtellinie große Fensterflächen aufweist, die nahezu unumschränkte
Rundumsicht gewähren. Weit ausladende, feststellbare Türen erleichtern
das Ein- und Aussteigen von vorn wie hinten. Auf den anatomisch konsequent durchgeformten Einzelsitzen spürt man schon im Stand, wie
wichtig erst recht bei schnellen Wagen der oft vermißte Halt im Sitz
ist. So wie der prozentuale Nutzraum-Anteil für Fahrer und Insassen
einen Spitzenwert innerhalb der GT-Klasse darstellt, verhält es sich auch
mit dem großdimensionierten Gepäckraum unter der Vorderhaube.

1964

**When production
began in 1964 this
brochure appeared,
with the type number
changed to 911 at
Peugeot's request.**

NDARD EQUIPMENT

ows
c windshield washing system with automatic wiper
ion.
shield wipers with three speeds (controlled in three

interference-eliminating wiper motor.
vent windows with anti-theft security.
ent windows with anti-theft security.
are rear-view mirror.
d glass windshield.
window defroster.

ing
netrical anti-glare light (for all countries in which it
ack-up lights.
ment lighting adjustable without steps.
g lights.
ge space lighting.

ing system
rong-tone horns.
r lights.

ments
ometer with overall and daily odometers.
indicator.
auge with reserve warning light.
el gauge.
nperature gauge.
essure gauge.
tor lights for battery charging, high beams,
eter lights, blinker, hand brake, fog lights and

c clock with setting control.

cks
oors can be locked from outside, bolted from inside.
compartment lid locks.
of fuel filler cap opens only from inside.
g wheel lock combined with ignition lock.

or
ng ashtray.
lare dashboard with central wood paneling and
g above and below.
tte lighter (combined with plug for hand light).
hold for passenger on the inside of the door.
sts as pull-out handles.
ment points for seat belts.
ment clamps for luggage rack.
oat hooks at the edge of the roof.
added sun visors, with make-up mirror on the
ger side.
oor pockets to hold maps etc. and small loose
s.
wn seats.
g and fresh air ventilation.
eat backs fold down to form a luggage surface with
ide security.
ck behind the rear seats with anti-slide bar.
carpeting with heel protector panel on the driver's

towing ring.
c heating when car is parked.
ree constant ventilation through the roof lining.
proofing.
ouch-up stick.
production colors with six interior decor
nations.

SERIENMÄSSIGE AUSSTATTUNG

Scheiben
Elektrische Scheibenwaschanlage mit automatischer
Wischerbetätigung
Scheibenwischer mit drei Wischgeschwindigkeiten
(in drei Stufen regelbar)
UKW-entstörter Scheibenwischermotor
Ausstellfenster vorn mit Diebstahlsicherung
Ausstellfenster hinten mit Diebstahlsicherung
Abblendbarer Innenspiegel
Schichtglas für Frontscheibe
Heckfensterbeheizung

Beleuchtung
Asymmetrisches Abblendlicht (für alle Länder,
in denen es gesetzlich erlaubt ist)
Zwei Rückfahrscheinwerfer
Stufenlos regelbare Instrumentenbeleuchtung
Zwei Nebelleuchten
Kofferraumbeleuchtung

Signalanlage
Zwei Starktonhörner
Lichthupe

Instrumente
Geschwindigkeitsmesser mit Gesamt-Kilometerzähler und
Tages-Kilometerzähler
Drehzahlmesser
Benzinuhr mit Restanzeigeleuchte
Ölstandmesser
Öltemperaturmesser
Öldruckmesser
Kontrolleuchten für Batterie-Ladestrom, Fernlicht, Begrenzungs-
licht, Blinker, Handbremse, Nebelleuchten, Heizung
Elektrische Zeituhr mit Zeitfeststeller

Schlösser
Beide Türen von außen abschließbar, von innen verriegelbar
Handschuhkasten abschließbar
Verschlußdeckel für Benzinfüllstutzen nur von innen zu öffnen
Lenkradschloß mit Zündschloß kombiniert

Interieur
Schiebeascher
Oben und unten gepolstertes blendfreies Armaturenbrett mit
mittlerer Holzabdeckung
Zigarrenanzünder (kombiniert mit Anschluß für Handleuchte)
Haltegriff für Beifahrer an der Türinnenseite
Armstützen als Zuziehgriffe
Befestigungsstellen für Sicherheitsgurte
Befestigungskrampen für Kofferriemen
Zwei Kleiderhaken am Dachrahmen
Zwei gepolsterte Sonnenblenden, auf der Beifahrerseite mit
Make-up-Spiegel
Zwei Türtaschen zur Unterbringung von Landkarten etc. und
kleinen sperrigen Gegenständen
Liegesitze
Heizung und Frischluftzuführung
Fond-Sitzlehnen als Gepäckauflage umklappbar mit
Rutschsicherungsleiste
Hutablage hinter den Fondsitzen mit Rutschsicherungsleiste
Veloursteppich mit Absatzschonerplatte auf der Fahrerseite

Sonstiges
Abschleppöse vorn
Benzinelektrische Standheizung
Zugfreie Dauerbelüftung durch die Dachverkleidung
Entdröhnung
1 Lackstift
7 Serienfarben mit 6 Innenausstattungskombinationen

At first there was only the coupe with a 130-hp motor,producing its power with a displacement of scarcely two liters.

in upper box

Schematic drawing of the heating

Da die Belüftung des Wageninneren wesentlich zum Wohlbefinden des Fahrzeuginsassen beiträgt, wurde ihr besondere Aufmerksamkeit geschenkt. Zum Beispiel wird der Innenraum durch Absaugschlitze über der Heckscheibe zugfrei entlüftet. Der 911 verfügt serienmäßig über eine Motorheizung u n d eine benzinelektrische Heizung!

① Schlitze im Heckdeckel
② Axialgebläse
③ Entnahmestutzen
④ Wärmetauscher
⑤ Abgasleitungen
⑥ Abgasschalldämpfer
⑦ Verbindungsschläuche
⑧ Klappenkästen
⑨ Heizrohre
⑩ Schalldämpfer
⑪ Entfrosterdüse für Windschutzscheibe
⑫ Entfrosterdüse für Heckscheibe
⑬ Schieber
⑭ Frischluftanlage
⑮ Schwenkgriff
⑯ Fremdheizung
⑰ Lufteintritt für Fremdheizung

The 911 was not conceived as an uncompromising sports car; good interior ventilation was taken for granted.

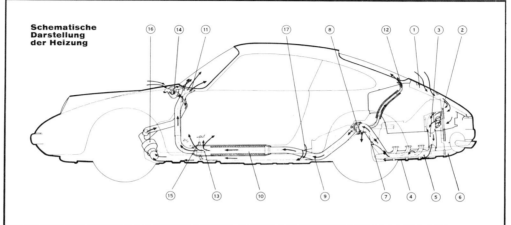

Schematische Darstellung der Heizung

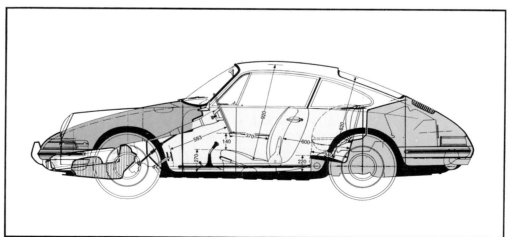

Since the ventilation of the car's interior contributes essentially to the comfort of the vehicle's passengers, particular attention has been given to it. For example, the interior is ventilated without a draft by the exit louvers above the rear panel. The 911 has standard motor heating *and* gas-electric heating.

1. Louvers in rear hood.
2. Axial blower.
3. Exit braces.
4. Heat exchanger.
5. Exhaust pipes.
6. Exhaust muffler.
7. Connection ducts.
8. Hatch boxes.
9. Heat ducts.
10. Noise dampers.
11. Windshield defroster duct.
12. Rear window defroster duct.
13. Lever.
14. Fresh air vents.
15. Control lever.
16. External heater.
17. Air intake for external heater.

Motor

Cylinders: 6
Bore: 80 mm
Stroke: 66 mm
Displacement: 1991 cc
Compression ratio: 9:1
Horsepower: 130 at 6100 rpm
Torque: 17.8 at 4200 rpm
Horsepower per liter: 65

Motor Construction

Type: air-cooled four-stroke Otto motor with horizontally opposed banks of three cylinders (boxer design).
Cylinders: Biral (cast iron pistons with light metal rings)
Cylinder head: light metal
Valves per cylinder: one inlet and one exhaust
Valve arrangement: V-formed, dropped
Valve activation: one overhead camshaft on each bank of cylinders
Camshaft drive: by chain
Crankshaft: forged, eight bearings
Connecting rod bearings: sliding bearings
Fan drive: by belt over generator
Lubrication: dry-sump
Fuel feed: 1 electric fuel pump, 1 mechanical double pump

Electric System

Voltage: twelve volts
Battery capacity: 45 Ah
Ignition: battery ignition
Spark plugs: Bosch W 250 P 21 (platinum)

Power Transmission

Motor position: in rear, behind the rear axle
Clutch: single-plate dry coupling
Gearbox: Porsche synchronized transmission
Number of gears: 5 forward, 1 reverse
Shift lever location: next to driver's seat on frame tunnel
Axle drive: spiral gear drive with bevel wheel differential
Power transmission: to the rear wheels via half-axles

Chassis and Suspension

Frame: pressed and welded sheet steel box frame with welded components
Front suspension: wheels independently sprung on springs and transverse links
Wheel suspension: one round longitudinal pushrod per wheel
Rear suspension: wheels independently sprung on longitudinal links, drive via half-axles
Wheel suspension: one round transverse pushrod per wheel
Shock absorbers: double-acting front and rear hydraulic
Foot brake: hydraulic, acting on all four wheels; disc brakes on all four wheels
Hand brake: mechanical, acting on the rear wheels, duo-servo brake drums
Effective braking diameter: front 235 mm, rear 243 mm
Brake surface per wheel: front 52.5 cc, rear 40.0 cc
Active braking area (foot brake): 185 cc
Hand brake drum diameter: 180 mm
effective braking area (hand brake): 194 cc
Wheel rims: 4.5 J x 15
Tires: 165 HR 15
Steering: ZF steering gear with hydraulic

Capacities

Motor: approx. 9.5 quarts oil, summer SAE 30, winter SAE 20
and differential: approx. 2.5 quarts Hypoid SAE 90
Fuel tank: 16.25 gallons, including approx. 1.5-gallon reserve (premium)

Dimensions

Wheelbase: 2211 mm
Front track: 1337 mm
Rear track: 1317 mm
Length: 4163 mm
Width: 1610 mm
Height (unladen): 1320 mm
Ground clearance: 150 mm
Turning circle: approx. 10.3 meters

Weights

Dry weight: 2376 lbs.
Gbe gross weight: 3080 lbs.

Performance

Top speed: 130 mph
power-to-weight: 19 lbs. per horsepower (1 person + dry weight)
Consumption: 2.5 gallons per 62 miles

Qualität durch Erfahrung — das war bei der Entwicklung des Typs 911 der Grundsatz der Porsche-Konstrukteure.

Ein exklusiver in allen Geschwindigkeitsbereichen ideal abgestufter Reisewagen verwandelt sich, zügig gefahren, in ein sportliches Coupé europäischer Elite.

Nicht Transport oder Repräsentation, sondern das beglückende Gefühl — Fahren um des Fahrens willen — begründet die alte Porsche-Formel „Fahren in seiner schönsten Form".

Excellence through experience — the maxim guiding Porsche designers in their work on Type 911.

An exclusive touring car, with its perfectly graduated speed ranges, it converts into a sporting coupe of the European elite.

The traditional Porsche slogan "Driving at its finest" expresses not simply the quality of movement or mechanism, but the joy of driving for its own sake.

La qualité grâce à l'expérience — tel fut le principe fondamental des usines Porsche lors de l'étude du type 911.

Une voiture de tourisme exceptionnelle, idéale et bien adaptée à tous les régimes, se transforment, lorsqu'elle est conduite rapidement, en un coupé sportif de standing européen.

Ce n'est pas son côté utilitaire ni son bel aspect, mais la sensation merveilleuse éprouvée à «conduire pour la joie de conduire» qui a créé le vieux slogan de Porsche: «Joie de conduire dans sa plus belle expression».

S-UL 837

Motor

Zylinderzahl		6
Bohrung	(mm)	80
Hub	(mm)	66
Hubraum tatsächlich	(cm³)	1991
Verdichtungsverhältnis		9:1
Leistung	(PS nach DIN)	130 bei 6100 U/min.
Höchstes Drehmoment	(mkp)	17,8 bei 4200 U/min.
Literleistung	(PS/l)	65

Motorkonstruktion

Bauart: luftgekühlter Viertakt-Ottomotor mit je drei sich gegenüberliegenden Zylindern (Boxer-Bauweise)
Zylinder: Biral (Grauguß-Büchse mit Leichtmetall-Kühlrippen)
Zylinderkopf: Leichtmetall
Anzahl der Ventile je Zylinder: 1 Einlaßventil und 1 Auslaßventil
Anordnung der Ventile: V-förmig, hängend
Ventilsteuerung: je eine obenliegende Nockenwelle auf jeder Zylinderreihe
Nockenwellenantrieb: durch Kette
Kurbelwelle: geschmiedet, 8 Gleitlager
Pleuellager: Gleitlager
Gebläseantrieb: durch Keilriemen über Lichtmaschine
Schmierung: Trockensumpfschmierung
Kraftstoff-Förderung: 1 elektr. Kraftstoffpumpe, 1 mech. Doppelpumpe
Vergaser: Solex-Überlaufvergaser, 3 pro Seite zusammengefaßt, Typ 40 PI

Elektrische Anlage

Nennspannung: 12 V
Batteriekapazität: 45 Ah
Zündung: Batteriezündung
Zündkerzen: Bosch W 250 P 21 (Platinkerze)

Kraftübertragung

Lage des Motors im Fahrzeug: im Heck hinter der Hinterachse
Kupplung: Einscheiben-Trockenkupplung
Schaltgetriebe: Porsche-Sperrsynchrongetriebe
Anzahl der Gänge: 5 vorwärts, 1 rückwärts
Schalthebel-Anordnung: neben Fahrersitz am Rahmentunnel
Achsantrieb: spiralverzahntes Kegelradgetriebe mit Kegelradausgleichgetriebe
Kraftübertragung: über Halbachsen auf die Hinterräder

Fahrgestell, Radaufhängung

Rahmen: Gepreßter und geschweißter Stahlblech-Kastenrahmen mit Aufbau verschweißt
Vorderradaufhängung: Einzeln an Federbeinen und Querlenkern aufgehängte Räder
Vorderradfederung: je Rad ein runder Drehstab in Längsrichtung liegend
Hinterradaufhängung: Einzeln an Längslenkern aufgehängte Räder. Antrieb über Halbachsen
Hinterradfederung: je Rad ein runder Drehstab quer liegend
Stoßdämpfer: vorn und hinten doppeltwirkend, hydraulisch
Fußbremse: hydraulisch, auf alle vier Räder wirkend. Scheibenbremsen an allen vier Rädern
Handbremse: mechanisch, auf die Hinterräder wirkend. Duo-Servo-Trommelbremse
Wirksamer Bremsscheiben-ø: vorn 235 mm ø, hinten 243 mm ø
Bremsfläche je Rad (Fußbremse): vorn 52,5 cm², hinten 40,0 cm²
Wirksame Bremsfläche gesamt (Fußbremse): 185 cm²
Handbrems-Trommel-ø: 180 mm
Wirksame Bremsfläche gesamt (Handbremse): 194 cm²
Felgen: 4,5 J x 15
Reifen: 165 HR 15
Lenkung: ZF-Zahnstangenlenkung mit hydraulischem Lenkungsdämpfer

Füllmengen

Motor: ca. 9 Liter Marken HD-Öl, Sommer SAE 30, Winter SAE 20
Getriebe mit Ausgleichgetriebe: ca. 2,5 Liter Hypoid SAE 90
Kraftstoffbehälter: 62 Liter, davon ca. 6 Liter Reserve (Super)

Abmessungen

Radstand: 2211 mm
Spurweite vorn: 1337 mm
Spurweite hinten: 1317 mm
Länge: 4163 mm
Breite: 1610 mm
Höhe (unbelastet): 1320 mm
Bodenfreiheit: 150 mm
Wendekreis: ca. 10,3 m

Gewichte

Leergewicht nach DIN: 1080 kp
Zulässiges Gesamtgewicht: 1400 kp

Fahrleistungen

Höchstgeschwindigkeit: 210 km/h
Leistungsgewicht: 8,8 kp/PS (1 Person + Leergewicht nach DIN)
Kraftstoff-Normverbrauch: 9,6 Liter/100 km (nach DIN)

1965

Sicherheits-gepolstertes Armaturenbrett, Transistordrehzahlmesser, Gesamt- und Tageskilometerzähler, elektrische Benzinuhr, Öl-Thermometer, Ölstandanzeiger, Öldruckmesser, Kontrolleuchten für Batterieladestrom, Fernlicht, Begrenzungslicht, Blinker, Handbremse. Elektrische Zeituhr, 3stufiger Scheibenwischer, Zigarrenanzünder, Lichthupe. Handschuhkasten mit Magnetverschluß und verschließbar. 4-Speichen-Holzlenkrad, Armstützen, Haltegriff für Beifahrer, verstellbare Vordersitze als Liegesitze ausgebildet, 2 Hecksitze im Fond als Gepäckauflage umklappbar, Lenkradschloß, 2 gepolsterte Sonnenblenden (für Beifahrer mit Make-up-Spiegel), Türtaschen beidseitig, Heckscheibenbeheizung, benzinelektrische Zusatzund Standheizung, Kofferraum 200 Liter.

Safety cushioned dashboard · transistorized tachometer · speedometer incorporating total and trip distance recorder · electric fuel gauge · oil gauge · oil temperature gauge · oil pressure gauge · pilot lamp for generator, high beam, parking lights, turn signal, handbrake · electric clock · 3-speed windshield wiper · cigarette lighter · headlight signal · lockable glove compartment with magnet · 4-spoked wood rim steering wheel · arm rests · passenger grab handle · adjustable front seats are fully reclining · two occasional rear seats are changeable into luggage space · steering column lock · 2 cushioned sun visors with a make-up mirror for passenger · map pocket in each door · rear window ventilation · engine heating system and gasolineelectric heater · luggage compartment 7 cu. ft.

Tableau de bord rembourré, compte-tours électronique, compteur kilométrique journalier et totalisateur, jauge d'essence électrique, thermomètre d'huile, indicateur de niveau d'huile, manomètre de pression d'huile, lampes-témoin de: charge de batterie, phares, feux de position, clignotants, frein à main. Montre électrique, essuie-glace à 3 vitesses, allume-cigare, avertisseur lumineux, boîte à gants avec fermeture magnétique et serrure, volant en bois à 4 rayons, accoudoirs, poignée pour passager, sièges AV réglables en forme de couchettes, 2 sièges à l'arrière, rabattables pour bagages, serrure de sécurité sur volant, 2 pare-soleil rembourrés (avec miroir pour passager), 2 vide-poches latéraux (dans les portières), chauffage de la glace arrière, chauffage à essence supplémentaire, utilisable à l'arrêt, commandé électriquement, capacité du coffre 200 litres.

Complete instrumentation and comfortable sport seating were part of the 911's equipment.

Luftgekühlter Boxer-Heck-Motor, Hubraum 1991 ccm,
6 Zylinder, 8fach gelagerte Kurbelwelle, 130 PS bei
6100 U/min. Einzelzylinderköpfe, hängende Ventile, obenliegende Nockenwellen, Nockenwellenantrieb durch Ketten,
automatische Kettenspannung, 6 Vergaser mit 2 gemeinsamen Schwimmergehäusen, Trockensumpf-Schmier-
system, Ölkühler mit thermostatischer Regulierung,
12-Volt-Drehstrom-Lichtmaschine mit verlängerter Achse
zum Antrieb des Axialgebläses,
Einscheiben-Trockenkupplung.
5Vorwärtsgänge,Porsche-Synchronisierung,wartungsfreie
Hinter- und Vorderachse durch Federstäbe abgefedert,
hohe Kurvenfestigkeit durch zusätzlichen Stabilisator,
Zahnstangenlenkung, Sicherheitslenksäule, Scheibenbremsen wartungsfrei, automatische Nachstellung,
Handbremse als Trommelbremse mit hohem Wirkungsgrad,
Gürtelreifen 165 HR 15.

Air-cooled horizontally opposed six cylinder engine
at rear of car · displacement 1991 cc · eight-bearing
crankshaft · 148 HP (SAE) at 6100 rqm · individual
cylinder heads · overhead valves · overhead camshafts ·
camshaft drive through chains · automatic chain
tensioning · 6 carburetors with 2 common float housings ·
dry sump lubrication · thermostat-controlled
oil cooler · 12 volt three-phase generator with integral
axial fan drive · single plate dry clutch ·
5 forward speeds · Porsche synchronization ·
maintenance-free front and rear axle, suspension by
torsion bars · high cornering stability through
additional anti-roll bar · rack and pinion steering ·
safety steering column · maintenance-free disk brakes ·
self-adjusting devices · handbrake designed as
drum brake · braced tread tires 165 HR 15.

Moteur arrière à essence, refroidi par air, cylindrée
1991 cm³, 6 cylindres, vilebrequin sur 8 paliers, 130 CV
à 6100 t/min., culasses séparées, soupapes et arbres à
cames en tête, entraînement des arbres à cames par
chaîne, réglage automatique de la tension de la chaîne,
6 carburateurs et 2 chambres de flotteur, système de
graissage à carter sec, radiateur d'huile à réglage
thermostatique, dynamo à courant triphasé 12 volts,
avec arbre prolongé pour l'entraînement de la soufflerie
axiale, embrayage monodisque à sec, 5 vitesses AV,
synchronisation Porsche, essieux AV et AR,
ne nécessitant pas d'entretien, avec barres de
torsion, très bonne stabilité dans les virages grâce à
un stabilisateur supplémentaire, direction à crémaillère,
colonne de direction de sécurité, freins à disque sans
entretien, réglage automatique, tambour sur frein à
main à grande efficacité, pneus ceinturés 165 HR 15

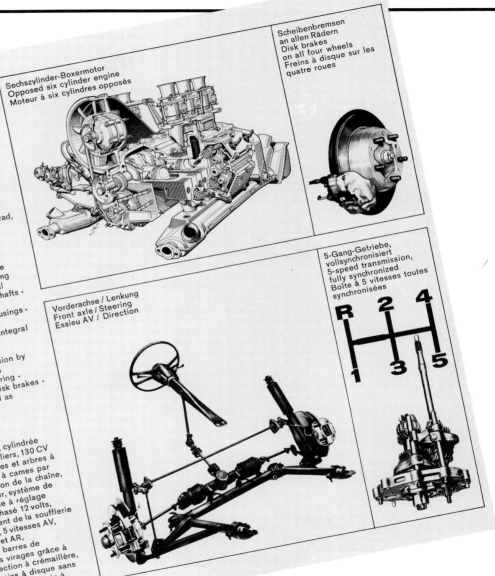

Sechszylinder-Boxermotor
Opposed six cylinder engine
Moteur à six cylindres opposés

Scheibenbremsen
an allen Rädern
Disk brakes
on all four wheels
Freins à disque sur les
quatre roues

Vorderachse / Lenkung
Front axle / Steering
Essieu AV / Direction

5-Gang-Getriebe,
vollsynchronisiert
5-speed transmission,
fully synchronized
Boîte à 5 vitesses toutes
synchronisées

R 2 4
1 3 5

Die Karosserieform kann man als greifbaren Beweis dafür ansehen, daß die schöpferische Begabung auch in der dritten Porsche-Generation weiterlebt.

Dieses rassige Coupé mit seinem grazilen Äußeren stellt ein Optimum aller Eigenschaften und Vorzüge dar, die der anspruchsvolle Porsche-Kunde seit Erscheinen des ersten Porsche-Wagens gewöhnt war.   Fahren in seiner schönsten Form—auch morgen.

The body style can be regarded as tangible proof that creative talent lives on in the third Porsche generation. This thoroughbred coupe with its graceful exterior offers an optimum of all characteristics and advantages that the exacting Porsche customer has become accustomed to since the appearance of the first Porsche car. Driving in its most beautiful form—tomorrow, too.

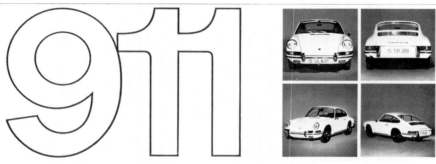

The body, harmonious from every angle, was designed by Porsche's grandson "Butzi."

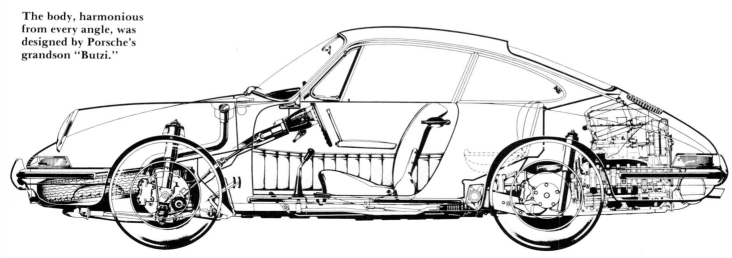

In September of 1965
the open version of the
911, called "Targa,"
was presented. Not a
convertible, but more
than just a car with a
sliding roof.

targa

Targa Florio, traditionsreiches Langstreckenrennen in den sizilianischen Bergen. Sizilianischer Frühling, südliche Sonne, sommerliche Temperaturen. Das italienische Wort „Targa" bedeutet auf deutsch „Schild": Der Sicherheitsbügel stellt einen echten Schutzschild für die Fahrgäste dar. Völlig neue Variationsmöglichkeiten, die weit über den herkömmlichen Komfort von Cabriolets hinausgehen, sind gegeben:

Die völlig offene Version, d. h. ohne Dach mit heruntergeklappter Heckscheibe, wird karosseriemäßig geprägt durch den Sicherheitsbügel und erhält dadurch eine neue stilistische Note, ein völlig neues Gesicht. Das Auto gewährleistet ein Höchstmaß an Sicherheit und gleichzeitig alle Annehmlichkeiten eines echten, offenen Sportwagens, in dem man Sommersonne und Sternenhimmel genießen kann.

Mit einem festen Dachaufsatz, der farblich auf den Lack des Wagens abgestimmt ist, wird der Targa zum Hardtop. In Minutenschnelle wird dieser Aufsatz mit einem Schnellverschluß am Sicherheitsbügel und der Windschutzscheibe befestigt. Durch die großflächige, durchsichtige Heckscheibe wirkt der Innenraum erheblich heller und freundlicher als man dies bisher bei einem Hardtop gewohnt war.

Anstelle des festen Dachaufsatzes gibt es ein zusätzliches zusammenklappbares Schnelldach für die Reise, das bei Sonnenschein zusammengerollt im Wagen liegt und bei Wetterumsturz zwischen Bügel und Windschutzscheibe eingespannt wird.

Man kann entweder die Heckscheibe am Platz lassen und ohne Dach, wie mit einem Riesenschiebedach fahren und Luft und Sonne von oben genießen, oder man läßt das Dach am Platz und löst mit einem einzigen Reißverschluß-Griff die Heckscheibe. Auf diese Weise sitzt man im Schatten und gleichzeitig im angenehmen Fahrtwind, eine Möglichkeit, die man vor allem bei extremen Hitzeverhältnissen in südlichen Ländern schätzen wird.

Targa Florio—tradition-rich long-distance auto race in the Sicilian mountains. Sicilian spring, southern sun, summery temperatures. The Italian word "Targa" means "shield." The roll bar represents a real safety shield for the passengers. Completely new variations are offered, far beyond the comfort formerly found in convertibles.

The completely open version, without roof and with lowered rear window, is characterized in form by the roll bar and thus strikes a new stylistic note, a fully new appearance. The car offers the maximum in safety and at the same time all the pleasures of a true open sports car, in which one can enjoy summer sun and starry skies.

With a closed roof, its color determined by that of the body, the Targa becomes a hardtop. This component is attached in minutes by quick fasteners on the roll bar and windshield. Thanks to the large-surface transparent rear window, the interior has a noticeably brighter, friendlier effect than one previously has been accustomed to in a hardtop.

In place of the solid roof, there is an additional folding roof, quickly raised, that is rolled up in the car for a trip in sunshine and erected between the roll bar and windshield if the weather changes.

One either can leave the rear window in place and travel without the roof, as if having a gigantic opening roof panel, and enjoy air and sun from above, or leave the roof in place and loosen the rear window with a single zipper attachment. In this way one sits in the shade and has a pleasant breeze at the same time, a possibility that one particularly will treasure in extremely hot weather in southern lands.

It was not difficult to present the car effectively
for advertising purposes.

In 1967 came the Type 911 S with 160-hp motor and typical, striking light metal wheels.

The 911 body was perhaps not stylish, but still timelessly elegant, meant to be built for a long time.

The striking wheels formed a stark contrast to the pragmatic bodywork; the 911 S could exceed 137 mph.

PORSCHE

Komfort

The interior not only is so extensive that driver and passenger can move comfortably; it also is possible for additional passengers to sit in the back for short distances. Two children (up to the age of about eleven) can sit comfortably in back even for long trips. If the rear seats are not needed, the seat back can be folded forward.

Technik im Detail

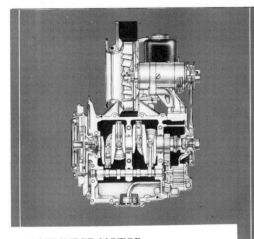

4-CYLINDER MOTOR

The motor is an air-cooled four-stroke Otto motor in boxer form, with 1.6-liter displacement. The forged crankshaft has four bearings in its light metal crankcase. Each pair of individual cylinders are attached to the left and right sides of the crankcase with a heavily ribbed light metal cylinder head. The dropped valves are arranged in V form and activated by pushrods and rocker arms from a camshaft. The camshaft is driven by gears from the crankshaft. Two carburetors supply the cylinders with fuel mixed with air. The motor oil is moved to the lubricating points by a gear-driven oil pump and cleaned by an oil filter. A thermostatically regulated oil cooler assures the correct oil temperature and protects the oil from overheating. The generator and cooling fan are driven by a V belt. Power transmission from motor to gearbox is expedited by a single-plate dry clutch.

GEARBOX

The gearbox forms a single unit with the differential. All forward gears are synchronized. The Porsche synchronization, with its servo effect, guarantees the shortest shifting times.

SPORTOMATIC four-speed gears with hydrodynamic polar moment changer. The automatic unit activates the clutch for starting, changing gears and stopping. Using the shift lever selects the correct driving levels for city, overland and mountain driving. The Sportomatic transmission can, if desired, be built into all six-cylinder models.

1. Gearbox drive shaft
2. Clutch rod
3. Servo motor
4. Clutch
5. Guide wheel
6. Pump wheel
7. Turbine wheel
8. Changer housing
9. Disc to accompany changer

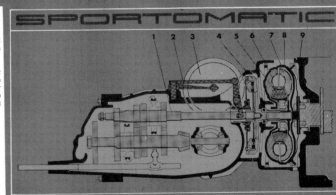

Left: The 911 still had two small back seats, but they were hardly meant for adults to ride in.

Especially for the USA, an important export market for Porsche, the semi-automatic Sportomatic transmission was offered optionally at the end of the sixties, eliminating the clutch.

Ausstattung

Das Mittelteil des Armaturenbretts der Typen 911 L und 911 S mit genarbtem Kunstleder verkleidet.

Charakteristisch für das äußere Bild des 911 S sind die geschmiedeten Leichtmetallfelgen. Ihr geringes Gewicht verbessert die Federungseigenschaften — die großen Luftöffnungen ermöglichen eine besonders intensive Belüftung der bei diesem leistungsstarken Fahrzeug härter beanspruchten Bremsen. Eine breite Leiste aus eloxiertem Leichtmetall unterhalb der Tür streckt das Fahrzeug optisch und verhindert Beschädigungen der Lackierung.

Felge für 911 S

Armaturenbrett für 911 L, 911 S
Radio nicht serienmäßig

911 S

SERIENMÄSSIGE AUSSTATTUNG 911 L / 911 S Elektrische Scheibenwaschanlage mit automatischer Wischerbetätigung · Scheibenwischer mit drei Wischgeschwindigkeiten · Wischerarme und Blätter blendfrei, schwarz mattiert · Ausstellfenster vorn und hinten* mit Diebstahlsicherung · Abblendbarer Innenspiegel · Mehrscheiben-Sicherheitsglas (Frontscheibe) · Defrosterdüsen an Front- und Heckscheibe* · Asymmetrisches Abblendlicht · Zwei Rückfahrscheinwerfer · Zweiklanghörner · Lichthupe · Geschwindigkeitsmesser mit Gesamt- und Tageskilometerzähler · Transistor-Drehzahlmesser · Benzinuhr mit Restanzeigeleuchte · Öltemperaturmesser · Kontrolleuchten für Batterie-Ladestrom, Öldruck, Begrenzungslicht, Fernlicht, Blinker, Handbremse · Elektrische Zeituhr mit Merkzeiger · Handschuhkasten mit Magnetverschluß, abschließbar · Vorderhaube, Motorhaube und Verschlußdeckel für Benzineinfüllstutzen nur von innen zu öffnen · Zwei gepolsterte Sonnenblenden (seitlich schwenkbar)*, für Beifahrer mit Make-up-Spiegel · Schiebeascher · Oben und unten gepolstertes blendfreies Armaturenbrett · Zigarrenanzünder (Anschluß für Handleuchte) · Schalttafelblende in Kunstleder „St" · Haltegriff für Beifahrer · Türtafel in Kunstleder mit „St"-Prägung · Zierleisten unter Ausstellfenstern und Türleisten innen · Armstützen als Zuziehgriffe · Zwei Klapptaschen unter Armlehnen · Befestigungsstellen für Sicherheitsgurte · Befestigungskrampen für Kofferriemen · Zwei flexible Kleiderhaken am Dachrahmen · Verstellbare Vordersitze (Liegesitze) · Zwei Hecksitze umklappbar, als Gepäckauflage verwendbar · Trittbrettleiste · Veloursteppich im Wagenraum, Farbe auf Kunstleder abgestimmt · Handgasbetätigung · Heizung und Frischluftzuführung stufenlos regulierbar · Zugfreie Entlüftung des Innenraumes durch Schlitze über der Heckscheibe · Befestigung für Abschlepphaken · Typenzeichen und Porsche-Schriftzug auf Motorhaube gold

* außer targa-Modelle

SERIENMÄSSIGE AUSSTATTUNG ZUSÄTZLICH BEIM 911 S Halogen-Nebellampen · Ölstandanzeiger · Öldruckanzeiger · Benzinelektrische Zusatz- und Standheizung mit separatem Gebläse · 4-Speichen-Lederlenkrad · Koni-Stoßdämpfer · Geschmiedete Leichtmetall-Felgen · Verstärkte Profilgummileisten zum Schutze der Stoßstangen und Stoßstangenhörner · Zierblende unterhalb der Türen

Wheel for the 911 S

The central section of the 911 L and 911 S dashboard, with grained leatherette covering.

Dashboard for 911 L and 911 S. Radio is not standard equipment.

911 S

Characteristic of the outer appearance of the 911 S are the forged light metal wheels. Their low weight improves the characteristics of the suspension—the large air intakes allow particularly intensive ventilation of this high-powered vehicle's brakes, on which high demands are made. A wide strip of light metal below the door stretches the body optically and prevents damage to the finish.

tric windshield washing system with automatic wiper
vation • three-speed windshield wipers • matt black non-
e wiper arms and blades • front and rear• vent windows
theft security • non-glare inside mirror • laminated safety
(windshield) • defroster ducts on windshield and rear
low • asymmetrical non-glare light • two back-up lights •
note horn • flashers • speedometer with overall and daily
neters • transistor rpm indicator • fuel gauge with reserve
ning light • oil temperature gauge • indicator lights for
ery charge, oil pressure, perimeter lights, high beams,
ers, hand brake • electric clock with readily visible hands •
e compartment with magnetic lid, lockable • front hood,
ne hood and filler cap lid released only from inside • two
led sun visors (swinging to the side), passenger's with
e-up mirror • ashtray drawer • non-glare dashboard
led at top and bottom • cigarette lighter (plug for hand
)* "St" leatherette gearshift panel cover • handhold for
enger • "St" leatherette door panels • interior trim strips
er vent windows and door frame • pull-out armrests •
belt attaching points • attaching rim for luggage rack •
flexible coat hooks on the roof frame • adjustable front
s (to lying position) • two foldable rear seats, usable for
ring luggage • footboard moulding • velour carpeting,
r-coordinated to leatherette • hand-activated accelerator •
ing and ventilation control (not stepwise) • draft-free
rior ventilation through louvers over the rear window •
ng hook attachment • gold type designation and Porsche
t on engine hood.

cept Targa models

DITIONAL STANDARD EQUIPMENT FOR THE 911 S

ogen fog lights • oil level indicator • oil pressure indicator
as-electric auxiliary and standing heater with separate
wer • 4-spoke leather steering wheel • Koni shock absorbers
rged light metal wheels • reinforced profiled rubber strips
rotect bumpers and bumper ends • trim panels under the

The standard equipment of the 911 S, which was very complete in this car in any case, even included standing heating.

Simple but artistic portrayals characterize the sales brochures of Porsche sports cars.

Linie, sondern vor allem den Insassen Sicherheit. Überdies ermöglicht er, mit wenigen Handgriffen, den Aufbau vierfach zu variieren und sich damit nach Belieben der jeweiligen Witterung anzupassen. Auch bei hohen Reisegeschwindigkeiten verhindert der Bügel weitgehend die sonst im offenen Fahrzeug übliche Belästigung durch Luftzug und Windgeräusche. Der **targa** gibt die Sicherheit und Geborgenheit des Coupés, wie auch die Freiheit des Cabriolets. Form und Funktion fanden im **targa** zu einer Porsche-typischen Synthese, die jeden Individualisten begeistert. Jedem Wunsch entsprechend, wird der **targa** in allen Modellversionen geliefert.

targa

...vielseitig und elegant, vier Wagen in einem ...

. . . lines, but above all safety for the oc Particularly the option of varying the upper ways and thus making it suit any weather. Eve speeds the roll bar prevents the annoyance of wind noise common in other open cars. T offers the safety and privacy of the coupe as w freedom of the convertible. Form and functio a synthesis typical of Porsche in the **targ** inspires every individualist. Answering every **targa** is available in all model versions.

. . . versatile and elegant, four cars in one

Although basically not a real convertible because of the massive roll bar, the Targa was preferred by a great number of Porsche drivers.

In the summer of 1968 this special brochure appeared, showing the Sportomatic transmission which allowed the driver to shift the four forward gears without declutching.

Two proven technical principles combined: fluid drive and a Porsche four-speed fully synchronized gearbox. Robust and simple in terms of construction and service. The Sportomatic consists of three essential elements: The fluid drive—also called hydraulic turning moment changing, automatic shifting and mechanical four-speed drive with parking lock.

The hydraulic turning-moment changer is built after the "Trilok Principle." Two cogwheels, the driving wheel (pump wheel) and the driven wheel (turbine wheel) are right next to one another in the changing housing. Between them the guide wheel runs on an idler, mounted on the gearbox housing and prevented from turning against the direction of the cogwheels.

The changing housing is filled under pressure by a pump with oil from the motor's oil reservoir. When the motor begins to turn the driving cogwheel, its cogs push the oil into the turbine wheel. Here the motion energy of the oil flow is transformed into power, and the turbine likewise begins to turn. When the oil now flows back out of the turbine wheel, the diagonal scoops of the guide wheel cause the oil to flow back to the pump wheel at a very favorable angle. An idler locates the guide wheel on the fixed gearbox housing and thus prevents it from turning in the opposite direction to the pump and turbine wheels. The deflection of the oil flow keeps the turning power transmitted from the motor to the pump wheel from being intensified in the turbine wheel. This intensification is greatest in a parked vehicle at the moment of starting to move, and is returned smoothly to a 1:1 ratio as driving speed increases.

Whenever the pump wheel turns faster than the turbine wheel because of increased motor speed, the deflection of the oil flow by the guide wheel affects the drive wheels with increasing power, i.e., in the form of increased turning moment. The greater the difference in the turning speeds of the two cogwheels, the stronger the effect. But after a short time the pump and turbine wheels run almost equally fast, and no intensification of the turning power takes place any more. The changer now works as a fluid coupling, and the guide wheel runs in the same direction as the two cogwheels. To change the gears mechanically, a separation of the power transmission between the motor and the changer on the one hand, and between the mechanical gears on the other hand, must both be made possible. Since at high engine speeds no interruption of power transmission is possible in the hydraulic changer, there is an automatic clutch between the changer and the mechanical gears. Since the car has no clutch pedal, it is activated by the partial vacuum in the motor's fuel intake line via a servo motor. The transmission of lowered pressure between this and the intake line is regulated by a control vent. Since wear on the gas pedal makes the static pressure in the fuel line weaker and turning off the motor makes it disappear altogether, the pressure is stored in a reservoir so that there always is a reserve on hand for several shifting processes.

A contact point on the shift lever gives the control vent an electrical impulse as soon as the shift lever is touched by the driver's hand.

1. Hydraulic turning moment changer
2. Clutch
3. Differential
4. Clutch rod
5. 4-speed gears
6. Parking lock

Zwei bewährte technische Prinzipien kombiniert: Das Strömungsgetriebe mit einem Porsche-Viergang-Vollsynchrongetriebe. Robust und einfach in Aufbau und Wartung. Die Sportomatic besteht aus drei wesentlichen Bauelementen. Dem Strömungsgetriebe – auch hydraulischer Drehmomentwandler genannt, der automatischen Schaltkupplung, dem mechanischen Vierganggetriebe mit Parksperre.

Der hydraulische Drehmomentwandler ist nach dem „Trilok-Prinzip" konstruiert. Zwei Schaufelräder, das treibende Schaufelrad (Pumpenrad) und das getriebene Schaufelrad (Turbinenrad) liegen sich im Wandlergehäuse dicht gegenüber. Zwischen ihnen läuft das Leitrad auf einem Freilauf, der sich am Getriebegehäuse abstützt und verhindert, daß es sich entgegen der Drehrichtung der Schaufelräder drehen kann.

Das Wandlergehäuse ist über eine Pumpe unter Druck mit Öl aus dem Motorenölreservoir gefüllt. Beginnt der Motor das treibende Schaufelrad zu drehen, dann drücken dessen Schaufeln das Öl in das Turbinenrad. Hier wird die Bewegungsenergie des Ölstromes in Kraft umgesetzt, und die Turbine beginnt sich ebenfalls zu drehen. Fließt nun das Öl aus dem Turbinenrad wieder zurück, so sorgen die schrägstehenden Schaufeln des Leitrades dafür, daß das Öl in einem sehr günstigen Winkel wieder in das Pumpenrad einfließt. Ein Freilauf stützt das Leitrad am feststehenden Getriebegehäuse ab und verhindert damit eine gegenläufige Drehbewegung des Leitrades zum Pumpen- und Turbinenrad. Die Umlenkung des Ölstromes bewirkt, daß die vom Motor auf das Pumpenrad übertragene Drehkraft im Turbinenrad verstärkt werden kann. Diese Verstärkung ist bei einem stehenden Fahrzeug im Moment des Anfahrens am größten und wird mit zunehmender Fahr-

geschwindigkeit stufenlos auf das Verhältnis 1 : 1 zurückgeführt.

Wann auch immer infolge einer Erhöhung der Motordrehzahl das Pumpenrad dem Turbinenrad voreilt, wird sich die Umlenkung des Ölstromes durch das Leitrad in zusätzlicher Kraft, d. h. erhöhtem Drehmoment, an den Antriebsrädern auswirken. Je größer die Differenz der Drehzahlen beider Schaufelräder, um so mehr wird der Effekt wirksam. Nach kurzer Zeit jedoch laufen Pumpen- und Turbinenrad nahezu gleich schnell, und es findet keine Verstärkung der Drehkraft mehr statt. Der Wandler arbeitet jetzt nur als Flüssigkeitskupplung, und das Leitrad läuft in gleicher Drehrichtung wie beide Schaufelräder.

Zum Wechsel der Fahrstufen im mechanischen Getriebe muß eine Trennung der Kraftübertragung zwischen Motor und Wandler einerseits und dem mechanischen Getriebe andererseits ermöglicht werden. Da bei höherer Motordrehzahl im hydraulischen Wandler keine Unterbrechung der Kraftübertragung möglich ist, befindet sich zwischen Wandler und mechanischem Getriebe eine automatische Schaltkupplung. Da das Kupplungspedal fehlt, wird sie durch den Unterdruck im Saugrohr des Motors über einen Servomotor betätigt. Der Unterdruckverlauf zwischen diesen und dem Saugrohr wird über ein Steuerventil geregelt. Da bei durchgetretenem Gaspedal der statische Unterdruck im Saugrohr nur schwach und bei abgestelltem Motor überhaupt nicht vorhanden ist, wird der Unterdruck in einem Reservebehälter gespeichert, damit stets noch Unterdruckreserven für einige Schaltvorgänge vorhanden sind.

Ein Kontaktgeber im Wählhebel gibt dem Steuerventil einen elektrischen Impuls, sobald der Wählhebel von der Hand berührt wird.

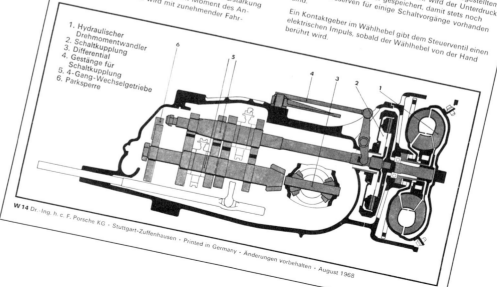

1. Hydraulischer Drehmomentwandler
2. Schaltkupplung
3. Differential
4. Gestänge für Schaltkupplung
5. 4-Gang-Wechselgetriebe
6. Parksperre

W 14 Dr.-Ing. h. c. F. Porsche KG · Stuttgart-Zuffenhausen · Printed in Germany · Änderungen vorbehalten · August 1968

FRONT AXLE: The independently sprung wheels are put in contact with shock absorbers via transverse links. The suspension functions by means of one adjustable longitudinal spring in the transverse link. In the 911 E the suspension and damping are taken over by a hydropneumatic spring which regulates its conditions independently. The 911 S also has an additional transverse stabilizer.

REAR AXLE: Independently sprung wheels, led by oblique links and sprung by adjustable transverse springs and a progressively acting hollow rubber spring. Damping works via hydraulic telescopic shock absorbers. Driving power is transmitted from the differential to the wheels through double-link shafts. All links are service-free. The 911 S additionally is equipped with a stabilizer.

VORDERACHSE: Die einzeln aufgehängten Räder werden durch Querlenker in Verbindung mit Stoßdämpferbeinen geführt. Die Federung erfolgt durch je einen, längsliegend im Querlenker angeordneten, einstellbaren Federstab. Beim 911 E wird die Federung und Dämpfung durch ein hydropneumatisches Federbein übernommen, das selbsttätig sein Niveau reguliert. Der 911 S erhält zusätzlich einen Querstabilisator.

HINTERACHSE: Einzeln aufgehängte Räder, die durch Schräglenker geführt und durch querliegende, einstellbare Federstäbe und eine progressiv wirkende Gummihohlfeder gefedert werden. Die Dämpfung erfolgt durch hydraulische Teleskopstoßdämpfer. Vom Ausgleichsgetriebe wird die Antriebskraft über Doppelgelenkwellen auf die Räder übertragen. Alle Gelenke sind wartungsfrei. Der 911 S ist zusätzlich mit Stabilisator versehen.

HEATING AND VENTILATION: All models have a new heating and ventilation system, which also is effective at slow speeds and with closed windows. The air warmed in the motor's heat exchanger can be mixed smoothly with cool fresh air and conducted to the head- or foot room as you wish.

A three-stage blower aids in air circulation, which can be moderated by louvers over the rear window (or vents in the Targa's roll bar). The rear windows are heated electrically. Air conditioning or gas-electric auxiliary heating can be connected to the heating-ventilation system.

HEIZUNG UND BELÜFTUNG: Alle Modelle weisen ein neues Heizungs- und Belüftungssystem auf, das auch bei niedriger Geschwindigkeit und geschlossenen Fenstern wirksam ist. Die im Wärmetauscher durch den Motor erwärmte Luft kann stufenlos mit zusätzlicher kühler Frischluft gemischt und beliebig in Kopf- oder Fußraum geleitet werden.

Ein Dreistufengebläse unterstützt den Durchsatz der Luft, die durch Schlitze über der Heckscheibe (beim targa durch Kiemen im Dachbügel) entweichen kann. Die Heckscheiben werden elektrisch beheizt. Eine Klimaanlage oder eine benzinelektrische Zusatzheizung kann an das Heizungs-Lüftungssystem angeschlossen werden.

Elegance
COMFORT
SAFETY
PERFORMANCE

The six-cylinder boxer motor of even the weakest 911 T version had the look of a rear racing motor with the six impressive air filters of the two three-barrel carburetors.

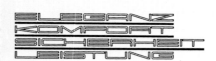

6-CYLINDER FUEL-INJECTION MOTOR 911 T

A robust throttle motor that need not avoid comparison with other sporting motors. From a displacement of 2 liters, it develops 110 hp at 5800 rpm. Characteristic is the great constant power over a wide range of engine speeds. Its six cylinders are set in boxer form (three each to the right and left of the crankcase) and attached to the strongly ribbed light metal cylinder heads. The hanging valves are set in V form and operated by one overhead camshaft per cylinder bank via rocker arms. The forged crankshaft has eight bearings. The mixture of fuel and air passes through a short intake pipe from the two three-barrel downdraft carburetors into the combustion chambers. Dry-sump lubrication guarantees the even supply of oil to the lubrication points (for example, at high cornering speeds), and the oil is cleaned in a mainstream filter and kept at the right temperature by an oil cooler. The three-phase current generator and axial fan for motor cooling are driven by V-belts.

6-ZYLINDER-VERGASERMOTOR 911 T

Ein robuster Drosselmotor, der dennoch kaum einen Vergleich mit anderen sportlichen Motoren zu scheuen braucht. Aus einem Hubraum von 2 Ltr. entwickelt er 110 PS bei 5800 U/min. Charakteristisch für ihn ist die große Durchzugskraft über einen weiten Drehzahlbereich. Seine 6 Zylinder sind in Boxerbauart (je drei rechts und links vom Kurbelgehäuse) angeordnet und mit den stark verrippten Leichtmetallzylinderköpfen verschraubt. Die hängenden Ventile sind V-förmig angeordnet und werden über Kipphebel durch je eine obenliegende Nockenwelle pro Zyli gesteuert. Die geschmiedete Kurbelwelle ist achtfach gelagert. Über kurze Saugrohre g Kraftstoff-Luft-Gemisch von den beiden Dreifach-Fallstromvergasern in die Verbre räume. Eine Trockensumpf-Schmierung garantiert die gleichmäßige Versorgung der S stellen mit Öl (z. B. bei hohen Kurvengeschwindigkeiten), das in einem Hauptstrom gereinigt und von einem Ölkühler auf der richtigen Temperatur gehalten wird. Dur riemen wird die Drehstromlichtmaschine und das Axialgebläse für die Motorkühlung an

BREMSEN: Alle Modelle sind mit einer Zweikreis-bremsanlage ausgestattet, die auf großdimensionierte Scheibenbremsen an allen Rädern wirkt und deren Bremssegmente sich automatisch nachstellen. Zur besseren Wärmeableitung, die vorzeitigem Verschleiß der Bremsbeläge vorbeugt, sind der 911 T mit „Sportomatic" sowie alle 911 E und 911 S mit innenbelüfteten Scheibenbremsen ausgestattet. Die Handbremse wirkt auf vom Scheibenbremssystem unabhängige Bremstrommeln der Hinterräder.

SICHERHEITSLENKUNG: Die Lenkbewegungen werden über eine abgewinkelte Lenksäule mit zwei wartungsfreien Kardangelenken auf eine direkt wirkende Zahnstangenlenkung übertragen, die symmetrisch hinter der Vorderachse angeordnet ist.

KAROSSERIE: Die selbsttragende, verwindungssteife Ganzstahlkarosserie ist mit der stabilen Bodengruppe zu einer Einheit verschweißt. Der verformungssteife Fahrgastraum wird durch nachgiebige Front- und Heckpartien, die Aufprallenergien verzehren, geschützt. Die Kotflügel vorn sind abschraubbar.
Alle Kabel, Leitungen und Betätigungsgestänge liegen geschützt im Rahmentunnel des geschlossenen Karosseriebodens.

NICHT ALLEIN DIE FAHRLEISTUNG ENTSCHEIDET ÜBER DEN WERT EINES WAGENS, SONDERN ZUVERLÄSSIGKEIT UND AUSGEWOGENHEIT ALLER KONSTRUKTIVEN DETAILS.

BRAKES: All models are equipped with a dual-circuit braking system, which operates large-dimension disc brakes on all wheels and whose braking elements are adjusted automatically. For better heat removal and to guard against premature wear of the brake pads, the 911 T "Sportomatic" and all 911 E and 911 S models are equipped with internally ventilated disc brakes. The hand brake operates rear-wheel drum brakes independent of the disc-brake system.

SAFETY STEERING: The steering motions are transmitted via an angled steering column with two service-free universal joints to a directly working rack-and-pinion system set symmetrically behind the front axle.

BODYWORK: The self-supporting, rigid all-steel body is welded to the stable bottom section to form a unit. The rigid passenger compartment is protected by deformable front and rear sections that absorb collision energy. The front fenders are removable.

All cables, connections and activators lie protected in the frame tunnel of the body's closed bottom.

NOT ONLY PERFORMANCE DECIDES THE VALUE OF A CAR, BUT RELIABILITY AND HARMONY OF ALL CONSTRUCTIVE DETAILS.

The arrangement of the instruments and controls in the 911's cockpit sets a model to this day; one immediately feels "at home" behind the wheel.

Maßstab für die Gestaltung und Ausstattung des Innenraumes ist: die leichte und schnelle Handhabung der Bedienungselemente, die Übersichtlichkeit aller Kontrollinstrumente, eine sinnvolle, die Konzentration des Fahrers fördernde und der Ermüdung vorbeugende Bequemlichkeit sowie die Sicherheit der Fahrzeuginsassen.
Der Innenraum ist so großzügig bemessen, daß Fahrer und Beifahrer gute Bewegungsfreiheit haben. Weitere Fahrgäste finden auf den Rücksitzen für kurze Strecken ebenfalls eine Sitzmöglichkeit. Werden die Rücksitze nicht benötigt, kann auf den nach vorn geklappten Sitzlehnen zusätzlich Gepäck verstaut werden.

Die tief, im Schwerpunkt des Wagens angeordneten vorderen Sitze stützen den Fahrer durch ihre Schalenform seitlich ab. Die anatomisch richtig geformten und vielfach verstellbaren Rückenlehnen beugen der Ermüdung auch auf langen Strecken vor.

Alle Kontrollinstrumente liegen blendfrei im Blickfeld des Fahrers. Die Bedienungsorgane sind klar angeordnet und leicht zugänglich. Ohne die Hände vom Lenkrad zu nehmen, kann der Fahrer über zwei Kombinationsschalter an der Lenksäule den dreistufigen Scheibenwischer, die Scheibenwaschanlage, Blinker, Lichthupe und Fernlichtumschaltung betätigen.

The measure of formation and equipment of the interior is the quick and easy handling of all operating controls, a sensible convenience that heightens the driver's concentration and avoids exhaustion as well as providing for the occupants' safety.

The interior dimensions are so great that the driver and passenger have good freedom of movement. Additional guests also have the possibility of sitting in the rear seats for short trips. When the rear seats are not in use, additional luggage can be stowed on the seat backs when they are folded down frontward.

The deep front seats, located at the car's center of gravity, support the driver to the sides by their cupped form. The adjustable seat backs, properly formed anatomically, help to avoid fatigue even on long trips.

All control instruments are in the driver's field of vision and are glare-free. The operating controls are easy to see and easy to reach. Without taking his hands off the wheel, the driver can use the two combination switches on the steering column to operate the three-speed windshield wipers, the windshield washing system, blinkers, flashers and high beams.

TECHNICAL DATA	COUPE/TARGA	912	911 T	911 E	911 S
MOTOR	cylinders	4	6	6	6
	bore	82.5 mm	80.0 mm	80.0 mm	80.0 mm
	stroke	74.0 mm	66.0 mm	66.0 mm	66.0 mm
	displacement	1582 cc	1991 cc	1991 cc	1991 cc
	compression ratio	9.3:1	8.6:1	9.1:1	9.9:1
	horsepower at rpm	90/5800	110/5800	140/6500	170/6800
	torque at rpm	12.4/3500	16/4200	17.8/4500	18.5/5500
	specific power	57 hp/l	55 hp/l	70 hp/l	85 hp/l
MOTOR CONSTRUCTION	type	air-cooled boxer with opposed cylinders			
	cylinders	4 Biral	6 cast iron	6 Biral	6 Biral
(Biral: cast iron w/light metal cooling fins)					
	cylinder heads	light metal			
	valves	1 intake, 1 exhaust per cylinder			
	valve position	dropped	V dropped	V dropped	V dropped
	valve action	1 camshaft, 1 camshaft on each bank, with pushrods and rocker arms rocker arms			
	camshaft drive gears	chain	chain	chain	chain
	crankshaft	forged, 4 bearings	forged, 8 bearings	forged, 8 bearings	forged, 8 bearings
	rod bearings	sliding			
	fan drive	V-belt via generator			
	lubrication	pressure	dry-sump	dry-sump	dry-sump
	fuel pump	mechanical	electric	electric	electric
	carburetors	2 double	1 3-barrel	Bosch fuel-injection	Bosch fuel injection
ELECTRIC	voltage	12 volts			
	generator	420-watt DC	770-watt 3 phase	770-watt 3 phase	770-watt 3 phase
	battery capacity	45 Ah	2x36 Ah	2x36 Ah	2x36 Ah
	ignition source	battery		battery (high-tension condensor ignition)	
	firing order	1/4/3/2	1/6/2/4/3/5	1/6/2/4/3/5	1/6/2/4/3/5
POWER TRANSMISSION	motor position	at rear, behind rear axle			
	clutch	1-plate dry clutch			
	gearbox	Porsche synchronized			
	gears	4+reverse	4+reverse	5+reverse	5+reverse
	shift lever position	central (on tunnel beside driver's seat)			
	axle drive	spiral geared bevel wheel and differential			
	axle ratio	7:31, i = 4.428			
	drive	to rear wheels via half-shafts			
CHASSIS AND SUSPENSION	frame	pressed and welded sheet steel box frame with welded superstructure			
	front suspension	wheels independently sprung on shock absorbers and transverse links			
	front springs	1 round longitudinal torsion bar/wheel; 911 S has additional stabilizer; 911 E has self-adjusting hydropneumatic suspension			
	rear suspension	wheels independently sprung on longitudinal links			
	rear springs	1 round transverse torsion bar per wheel; 911 S has additional stabilizer			
	shock absorbers	double-action hydraulic front and rear			
	foot brakes	dual circuit hydraulic disc brakes on all 4 wheels; 911 E and 911 S have internally cooled brake discs			
	hand brake	mechanical duo-servo drum brakes on rear wheels			

In 1967 there were four versions of the 911, of which the four-cylinder 912 version was produced for the European market only between 1965 and 1968.

TECHNICAL DATA	COUPE/TARGA	912	911 T	911 E	911 S
	front disc diameter	235 mm	235 mm	228 mm	228 mm
	rear disc diameter	244 mm	244 mm	244 mm	244 mm
	brake surface	52.5 cc	52.5 cc	76 cc	76 cc
	per wheel fr/rr	52.5 cc	52.5 cc	52.5 cc	52.5 cc
	total brake surface	210 cc	210 cc	257 cc	257 cc
	hand brake drum diameter	180 mm			
	hand brake surface	170 cc			
	wheel size	5.5 J x 15	5.5 J x 15	light metal 6 J x 15 (5.5 J x 14)	light metal 6 J x 15
	tires	165HR15	165HR15	185/70VR15 (185HR14)	815/70VR15
	steering	ZF rack-and-pinion			
GEAR RATIOS		1: 11:34	1: 11:34	1: 11:34	1: 11:34
		2: 19:32	2: 19:31	2: 18:34	2: 18:34
		3: 24:27	3: 25:26	3: 22:29	3: 22:29
		4: 28:24	4: 29:23	4: 25:26	4: 25:26
				5: 29:23	5: 29:23
CLIMBING POWER	vehicle weight	2486 lbs.	2662 lbs.	2662 lbs.	2640 lbs.
(dry weight plus half load)					
	1st gear climbs	46%	60%	68%	72%
	2nd gear climbs	21%	25%	34%	34%
	3rd gear climbs	12%	14%	21%	21%
	4th gear climbs	8%	8%	14%	15%
	5th gear climbs			8%	8%
CAPACITIES	oil	5.25 quarts HD	9.25 quarts HD	9.25 quarts HD	10.5 quarts HD w/oil cooler
	gearbox/differential	2.5 quarts			
	fuel tank	16.25 gallons			
	brake fluid tank	6 ounces			
	washer fluid	2 quarts			
DIMENSIONS	wheelbase	2268 mm			
	front track (with Sportomatic in parens.)	1362 mm	1362 mm	1374 mm (1364 mm)	1374 mm
	rear track (with Sportomatic in parens.)	1343 mm	1343 mm	1355 mm (1345 mm)	1355 mm
	length	4163 mm			
	width	1610 mm			
	height unladen	1320 mm			
	clearance loaded	150 mm			
	turning circle	about 10.7 m			
WEIGHTS	empty	2090 lbs.	2244 lbs.	2244 lbs.	2189 lbs.
	gross wt. limit	2860 lbs.	3080 lbs.	3080 lbs.	3080 lbs.
	max. front axle weight	1254 lbs.	1320 lbs.	1320 lbs.	1320 lbs.
	max. rear axle weight	1694 lbs.	1848 lbs.	1848 lbs.	1848 lbs.
(gross weight limit must not be exceeded)					
PERFORMANCE	top speed	115 mph	124 mph	134 mph	140 mph
	power to weight ratio	25 lbs./hp	22 lbs./hp	17 lbs./hp	14 lbs./hp
(1 person plus dry weight)					
	fuel consumption (for 62 miles)	2.25 gallons	2.4 gallons	2.5 gallons	2.75 gallons

As of 1968 the E and S models each gained ten horsepower by the addition of Bosch fuel injection.

The seats were made anatomically correctly and gave passengers safe lateral support even on sharp curves.

As for its driving characteristics, the early 911 was not exactly one of the easiest-controlled vehicles, as this picture is perhaps meant to show—or is it?

Seen from this
perspective too (above),
the 911 displays a good
figure. In 1969 the
motors were bored out
to displace 2.2 liters.

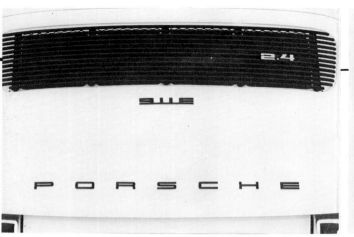

Ein Porsche liegt nicht nur in Leistung, Sportlichkeit und technischer Perfektion über dem Durchschnittsauto, sondern naturgemäss auch im Preis.

Und deshalb müssen viele, die von diesem Auto träumen, sehr lange träumen, ehe sie sich einen fabrikneuen Porsche leisten können.

Es spricht jedoch nichts dagegen, die Wartezeit abzukürzen, indem Sie zunächst mit einem Porsche aus zweiter Hand anfangen. Weil das Risiko dabei oft sogar geringer ist als bei anderen Gebrauchtwagen.

Denn in unserem weltweiten Service sorgen wir dafür, dass ein Porsche mit der gleichen Perfektion gewartet wird, mit der er gebaut ist.

Das hält ihn so robust und widerstandsfähig, wie man es nur von wenigen Fahrzeugen erwarten kann. Und kaum von einem Sportwagen.

A Porsche not only is above the average in performance, sportiness and techni[cal] perfection, but naturally in price too.

Therefore many who dream of this car m[ay] dream a long time before they can aff[ord] a factory-new Porsche.

But there is no reason not to shorten the waiting time by starting with a secondhand Porsche. For the risk involved often is less than with other used cars.

In our worldwide service we make sure th[at] a Porsche is maintained with the same perfection with which it is built.

That keeps it as robust and resistant as on[e] can expect from few cars.

And hardly from a sports car.

Es gibt weit mehr Leute, die sich einen Porsche 911 leisten können als Leute, die ihn sich leisten.

Wäre die Anschaffung eines Porsche lediglich eine Frage des Geldes, würden sich viel mehr Autofahrer einen Porsche kaufen.

Das liegt daran, daß man für dieses Auto etwas braucht, das seltener ist als ein mehrstelliges Bankkonto:

Auto-Verstand.

Wer den nicht hat, für den ist der Porsche allenfalls ein schicker Wagen, der auf der Autobahn alles hinter sich läßt, mehr nicht.

Daß der Porsche mehr ist – vielleicht eine automobiltechnische Welt für sich – lassen seine Technik, seine Leistungsdaten und sein Äußeres, das bis ins scheinbar unwesentlichste Detail vollkommen ist, erahnen.

Erfassen aber läßt sich ein Porsche erst, wenn man ihn fährt.

There are many more people who can afford a Porsche 911 as people who afford it.

If buying a Porsche were merely a matter of money, many more drivers would buy themselves a Porsche.

The reason is that one needs something for this car that is rarer than a multiple-figure bank account: Understanding of cars.

To whomever doesn't have that, the Porsche is, of course, a chic car that leaves everything else on the superhighway behind, and nothing more.

That the Porsche is more—perhaps a world of auto technology in itself—car[n] seen in its technology, performance da[ta] and exterior, which is complete to the seemingly most unimportant detail.

But a Porsche only can be understoo[d] when one drives it.

With very detailed advertising texts, this big catalog from the early seventies was meant to show the undeniable advantages of the 911.

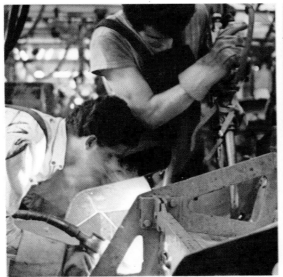

Above: Pictures showing specialist workers conscientiously assembling the cars were intended to inspire trust in the quality of these high-value sports cars.

Even after almost ten years of production, there had been no essential changes in the car's equipment. Racing success added a lot to the 911's dynamic image.

Die technische Vervollkommnung des Porsche 911 erklärt sich aus einer langjährigen Erfahrung mit diesem Fahrzeug, seiner Beobachtung im Alltagsverhalten und aus der Tatsache, dass wir Konstruktion und Details in Rennläufen immer wieder kritischen Erprobungen unterziehen.
Wenn Änderungen für die Serie vorgenommen wurden, fanden sie im Automobilsport härteste Erprobung. Nie aber musste der Porsche in seinem Grundkonzept geändert werden.
So macht ihn auch jetzt der 2,4 l-Motor nicht zu einem neuen, sondern zu einem besseren Porsche.
Heute, Jahre nach dem Erscheinen des ersten Porsche 911, vertreten wir noch immer die gleiche Einstellung zum Sportwagenbau: im Rennsport unsere Konstrukteure ständig mit neuen Problemen zu konfrontieren. Um Gutes durch Besseres zu ersetzen.

The technical completeness of the Porsche 911 is explained by long years of experience with this vehicle, its observation in everyday use, and the fact that again and again we put construction and details to critical tests in racing.

Whenever changes have been put into production, they have passed the hardest tests in automotive sports. But the Porsche's basic concept never has had to be changed. So the new 2.4-liter motor does not turn it into a new Porsche but into a better one.

Today, years after the first Porsche 911 appeared, we still represent the same outlook on sports car construction: to confront our constructors constantly with new problems in racing. To replace good with better.

A motor that will go
down in automotive
history since it
possesses astonishing
reliability despite its
high performance.

Every Porsche is new only when it is 22 miles old.

The more technically demanding a car is, the more thoroughly it should be tested. The Porsche must pass a whole series of stringent tests before it is released.

Just take its motor. Before it is assembled, every single part's quality is tested most precisely. The vents and camshafts, for example, are tested for weight, balance and firmness of material.

Every fully assembled motor is tested on the test bench for performance, ignition and consumption. Only then comes the last, decisive test for the finished vehicle—by the Porsche test drivers.

On driving test apparatus and then on a 22-mile-long test course, everything on the car— the performance of the motor, the power transmission, the suspension tuning, the steering precision, the braking system, the tire quality, and so on—is tested systematically for proper functioning one more time.

But the best test track—the race track—is already behind the Porsches before they are built.

Right: Before the cars reach the dealer, they are, as always, subjected to stringent testing, a procedure on which Porsche spends a good deal of time.

Jeder Porsche ist erst dann neu, wenn er 35 km alt ist.

Je technisch aufwendiger ein Wagen ist, desto gründlicher sollte er geprüft werden. Der Porsche muß erst eine ganze Reihe harter Tests bestehen, bevor er freigegeben wird.

Nehmen Sie nur seinen Motor. Bevor er zusammengesetzt wird, wird jedes einzelne Teil genauestens auf seine Qualität geprüft. Die Ventile und Nockenwellen zum Beispiel auf Gewicht, Unwucht und Materialfestigkeit.

Jeder fertig montierte Motor wird im Prüfstand auf Leistungsabgabe, Zündeinstellung und Verbrauch kontrolliert. Erst dann kommt für das fertiggestellte Fahrzeug die letzte, entscheidende Prüfung: Von den Porsche-Testfahrern.

Auf Fahrprüfständen und anschließend auf einer 35 Kilometer langen Teststrecke wird alles am Wagen noch einmal systematisch auf seine Funktionstüchtigkeit geprüft: Die Leistung des Motors, die Kraftübertragung, die Fahrwerkabstimmung, die Lenkgenauigkeit, die Bremsanlage, die Reifenqualität und so weiter.

Die beste Teststrecke indes haben die Porsche schon hinter sich, bevor sie gebaut werden: die Rennstrecke.

Das Fahrwerk erfüllt die Forderung einer optimalen Verbindung von sportlicher Sicherheit und Fahrkomfort.

Mit der Porsche Fahrwerkkonstruktion wird deutlich, daß Federungs- und Dämpfungskomfort keineswegs im Widerspruch zu sportlich stabilem Fahrverhalten stehen.

Die einzeln aufgehängten Vorderräder werden durch Querlenker in Verbindung mit Drehstabfedern und Stoßdämpfern geführt. Das bedeutet, daß die Räder unabhängig voneinander Kontakt zur Fahrbahn haben. Genauer: Schlaglöcher und Bodenwellen, die auf das eine Rad einwirken, lassen das andere unbeeinträchtigt in seiner Laufkonstanz.

Auch die hinteren Räder sind einzeln aufgehängt. Sie werden durch Schräglenker geführt und durch querliegende Federstäbe und doppelt wirkende hydraulische Stoßdämpfer gefedert. Gegen Aufpreis werden die Porsche mit Querstabilisatoren ausgerüstet (beim 911 S serienmäßig), die den Rädern einen noch besseren Kontakt mit der Straße ermöglichen.

Zur hohen Kurvengeschwindigkeit der Porsche-Modelle tragen auch die breiten Felgen und Reifen bei. Sie verstärken erheblich den Abstützeffekt des Fahrgestells, nehmen größere Seitenkräfte auf und ermöglichen eine höhere Querbeschleunigung.

Außerdem haben große Räder (bei allen Porsche 15 Zoll) mehr Umfang. Und damit den Vorteil, daß sie unfreundliche Strecken besser verkraften und die Reifen eine längere Lebensdauer haben.

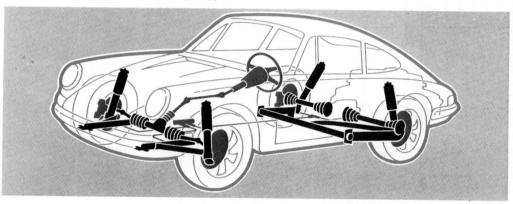

◀ 911 S mit Bugschürze als Spoiler ausgebildet.

—911 S with bow skirt built into a spoiler.

A carefully tuned chassis construction achieves a sufficient amount of comfort, despite the car's stiff springs.

The running gear fulfills the demand for an optimal union of sporting safety and riding comfort.

In the construction of the Porsche running gear, it becomes clear that suspension and damping comfort are not at all in opposition to sporting stability of handling.

The independently sprung front wheels are connected by transverse links to torsion bars and shock absorbers. That means that the wheels make contact with the road independently of one another. More precisely: potholes and bumps that affect one wheel let the other go its way smoothly, uninfluenced.

The rear wheels also are independently suspended. They are led by diagonal links and sprung by transverse springs and double-acting hydraulic shock absorbers. At extra charge the Porsche also can be equipped with transverse stabilizers (standard in the 911 S), which make possible even better contact of the wheels with the road.

The wide wheel rims and tires of the Porsche models also contribute to high cornering speeds. They considerably increase the supporting effect of the chassis, absorb great lateral force and make possible a higher cornering speed.

In addition, big wheels (15 inches on all Porsches) have a greater circumference. That gives them the advantage of handling unfriendly surfaces better and thus giving the tires a longer lifetime.

Its luggage space of 52.2-gallon capacity is more than doubled.

Sein Gepäckraum von 200 l Inhalt lässt sich auf mehr als das Doppelte vergrössern.

The space-saving front axle construction takes up so little room in the front of the body that the wide luggage space could hold contents of 52.5-gallon in volume.

It is fully lined with felt so your luggage won't slide back and forth or be damaged on the corners.

The rear engine made it possible for the Porsche 911 to have two additional seats. If the front luggage space is not enough, just reach behind you and fold the backs of these seats down. Thus a luggage space of about 62 gallons is created.

The Porsche 911 has as much room as a middle-sized sedan offers. That's very unusual for a sports car.

The well-conceived, space-saving front axle construction increased the front luggage space of the Porsche 911 considerably in comparison to that of its predecessor, the 356.

Die platzsparende Vorderachskonstruktion nimmt so wenig Raum im Vorderteil der Karosserie ein, daß der breite Kofferraum einen Inhalt von 200 l bekommen konnte.

Er ist voll ausgekleidet mit Nadelfilz, damit Ihr Gepäck nicht hin- und herrutscht und nicht an den Kanten beschädigt wird.

Durch den Heckmotor war es möglich, den Porsche 911 mit 2 Zusatzsitzen auszustatten. Und sollten Sie mit dem Kofferraum vorn nicht auskommen, greifen Sie einfach hinter sich und klappen die Lehnen dieser Sitze herunter. Dadurch entsteht noch ein Gepäckraum von ca. 235 l.

Insgesamt also soviel, wie eine Mittelklasse-Limousine bietet. Was für einen Sportwagen recht ungewöhnlich ist.

Alle Porsche haben jetzt einen Hubraum von 2,7 Liter. Als 911 mit 150 PS. Als 911 S mit 175 PS. Und als Carrera mit 210 PS. Schon bei niedrigen Drehzahlen liefern die Motoren ein hohes Drehmoment. Ein extrem kurzer Hub der luftgekühlten Sechs-Zylinder-Motoren in Boxerbauweise sorgt für niedrige Kolbengeschwindigkeiten, was sie robust, alltagsfest und langlebig macht. Die V-förmig hängenden Ventile werden über Kipphebel durch je eine obenliegende Nockenwelle pro Zylinderreihe gesteuert.

Die Auslaßventile sind natriumgekühlt. Beim 911 und 911 S sorgt eine neue Benzineinspritzung für die Gemischbildung: Die K-Jetronic. Sie arbeitet mit dem

Das neue Sechs-Zylinder-Triebwerk ist besonders elastisch und spurtstark.

Ansaugdruck des Motors. Und sie verringert erheblich die Schadstoffe in den Abgasen. Für die PS-stärkere Carrera-Version sorgt eine mechanisch angetriebene Einspritzung. Alle Porsche-Motoren kommen mit bleiarmem Normalbenzin aus. Die Kurbelwelle ist geschmiedet und achtfach gelagert. Die Trockensumpfschmierung garantiert allen Schmierstellen immer die erforderliche Menge Öl. Auch bei hohen Kurvengeschwindigkeiten.

Und das, was die Porsche in erster Linie so sportlich macht, macht sie schon in zweiter Linie so sicher. Die starke Beschleunigung. Die schnellen Bremsen. Das aufwendige Fahrwerk.

The new six-cylinder power plant is especially flexible and lively.

All Porsches now have a displacement of 2.7 liters. The 911 has 150 horsepower, the 911 S has 175, and the Carrera has 210. Even at low engine speeds the motors provide high torque. The extremely short stroke of the air-cooled six-cylinder boxer motors provides for low piston speeds, which makes them robust, ready for everyday use and long-lived. The V-shaped dropped valves are activated via rocker arms by one overhead camshaft per cylinder bank.

The exhaust valves are natrium-cooled. In the 911 and 911 S, a new fuel injection—the K-Jetronic—provides for fuel mixing. It works by the suction pressure of the motor and much decreases the pollutants in the exhaust. In the higher-horsepower Carrera version, the injection is mechanically driven. All Porsche motors can run on regular unleaded gasoline. The crankshaft is forged and has eight bearings. The dry-sump lubrication always guarantees all lubrication points the right amount of oil, even at high cornering speeds.

What makes the Porsche so sporting in the main also makes it so safe. The quick acceleration. The fast braking. The superb suspension.

The first Porsche Carrera with a 2.7-liter motor appeared in 1972, and one year later the other 911s also gained the increased displacement.

Die neuen Porsche 2,7 Liter. Es sind immer nur wenige, die sich das leisten, wovon andere träumen.

The new Porsche 2.7 liter. There always are just a few who can afford what others dream of.

Die Technik in Daten.

	911	911 S	Carrera
Motor			
Zylinder/Hubraum	6/2687 ccm	6/2687 ccm	6/2687 ccm
Bohrung/Hub	90/70,4 mm	90/70,4 mm	90/70,4 mm
Verdichtung	8,0 : 1	8,5 : 1	8,5 : 1
Oktanbedarf	91 ROZ (Normalbenzin)	91 ROZ (Normalbenzin)	91 ROZ (Normalbenzin)
Leistung	150 PS/5700 U/min	175 PS/5800 U/min	210 PS/6300 U/min
max. Drehmoment	24 mkp/3800 U/min	24 mkp/4000 U/min	26 mkp/5100 U/min
Gemischbildung	K-Jetronic	K-Jetronic	mech. Saugrohreinspritzung
Fahrgestell			
Vorderradaufhängung	Querlenker mit Dämpferbein u. Stabilisator	Querlenker mit Dämpferbein u. Stabilisator	Querlenker mit Dämpferbein u. Stabilisator
Hinterradaufhängung	einzeln an Längslenkern aufgehängte Räder	einzeln an Längslenkern aufgehängte Räder	einzeln an Längslenkern aufgehängte Räder
Fußbremse	Zweikreis-Vierradscheibenbremsen mit innenbelüfteten Bremsscheiben		
Elektr. Anlage			
Lichtmaschine	Drehstrom 770 W	Drehstrom 770 W	Drehstrom 770 W
Batterie	12 V/66 Ah	12 V/66 Ah	12 V/66 Ah
Felgen/Reifen	5 1/2J x 15/165 HR 15 Stahl	6J x 15/185/70 VR 15 Leichtmetall	vorn 6J x 15/185/70 VR 15, hinten 7J x 15/215/60 VR 15 Leichtmetall
Abmessungen			
Länge/Breite/Höhe	4291/1610/1320 mm	4291/1610/1320 mm	4291/1652/1320 mm
Gewichte			
Leergewicht	1075 kp	1075 kp	1075 kp
Zuladung	325 kp	325 kp	325 kp
Ausstattungsunterschiede			
Innen	Sportlenkrad Nadel-Velours-Teppiche	Sportlenkrad Spezial-Velours-Teppiche	Sportlenkrad, Leder Spezial-Veloursteppich, elektr. Fensterheber (Coupé)
Außen	Fenstereinfassungen etc. in Chrom	Fenstereinfassungen etc. in Chrom	Fenstereinfassungen etc. in mattschwarz
Fahrleistungen			
Höchstgeschwindigkeit	210 km/h	225 km/h	240 km/h
Beschleunigung 0-100 km/h	8,5 sec	7,6 sec	6,3 sec

In 1973 there were still three different models ranging from 150 to 210 horsepower, while the Carrera, with a top speed of some 150 mph, still had to fear few rivals.

VW-Porsche Vertriebsgesellschaft mbH · 714 Ludwigsburg · Porschestraße 15-19
Die abgebildeten Fahrzeuge sind teilweise mit Sonderausstattungen ausgerüstet und entsprechen nicht immer der angebotenen Grundausführung. Wir behalten uns vor, ohne Veröffentlichung Änderungen an Konstruktion und/oder Ausstattung vorzunehmen. Herausgeber: VW-Porsche Vertriebsgesellschaft mbH, Abt. Marketing-Werbung
1033.10 Printed in Germany · SVA, Ludwigsburg

The Porsche Carrera,
in a brochure intended
for the USA, with the
typical rear spoiler—a
novelty in the building
of production cars.

**The Porsche Carrera.
Inspiration for a New Porsche Generation.**

PORSCHE 911

The Porsche 911 is a phenomenon: already on the market 12 years—and still on top, externally changed only in details, but refined to unbeaten perfection.

What a forward-looking creation the 911 already was—and what a timeless one it is now as then—shown not only in the irresistable charm and in the constantly increasing popularity of this car, but also proved by hard data, numbers and facts.

The safety and emission tests required by the USA, which many consider too strict or downright unfulfillable, the Porsche passed at once and without the slightest change. Its high-performance motor is satisfied with (a little) regular gasoline, and only needs an inspection and oil change every 12,500 miles.

This minimum of maintenance and service is crowned by Porsche with the maximum in guarantees. As the leader in the concept of long-life automobiles, Porsche (the only manufacturer who does!) guarantees freedom from rust for six years—and thereby an unequaled lasting value and the highest possible reselling price.

Always timeless, always timely and always ahead of its time—these three qualities made the Porsche 911 the most successful among the world's classic sports cars (and the most pleasant for its owners).

Technical Data

Six-cylinder boxer motor, air-cooled, rear-mounted—power transmission via half-axles to the rear wheels—2.7-liter displacement—2687 cc—165 hp at 5800 rpm—K-Jetronic—8.5:1 compression—acceleration from 0 to 62 in 7.5 sec.—top speed over 130 mph—with Porsche's longtime guarantee.

PORSCHE 911

Der Porsche 911 ist ein Phänomen: schon 12 Jahre auf dem Markt – und immer noch an der Spitze; äußerlich nur in Details verändert, insgesamt jedoch zu unübertroffener Perfektion gereift.

Was für eine vorausschauende Konstruktion der 911 immer schon war – und was für eine zeitlose er nach wie vor ist – das zeigt sich nicht nur im unwiderstehlichen Reiz und in der ständig steigenden Beliebtheit dieses Autos, sondern das beweisen auch harte Daten, Zahlen und Fakten.

Die von den USA geforderten Sicherheits- und Umwelt-Tests, die viele für zu streng oder gar für unerfüllbar halten, bestand der Porsche auf Anhieb und ohne die geringste konstruktive Änderung. Sein Hochleistungsmotor begnügt sich mit (wenig) Normal-Benzin; und nur alle 20 000 Kilometer muß der Porsche zur Inspektion und zum Ölwechsel.

Dieses Minimum an Unterhalts- und Wartungsansprüchen krönt Porsche mit einem Maximum an Garantie: Als Schrittmacher der Idee des Langzeit-Autos bürgt Porsche (als einziger Hersteller überhaupt!) für sechs Jahre Rostfreiheit – und damit für eine beispiellose Werterhaltung und für höchstmögliche Erlöse beim Wiederverkauf.

Immer zeitlos, immer zeitgemäß und immer seiner Zeit voraus – diese drei Eigenschaften machten den Porsche 911 unter den klassischen Sportwagen der Welt zum erfolgreichsten (und seine Besitzer zu den zufriedensten).

Technische Daten

6-Zylinder-Boxermotor, luftgekühlt, hinten · Kraftübertragung über Doppelgelenkwelle auf die Hinterräder · 2,7 l Hubraum · 2687 ccm · 165 PS/121,5 kW bei 5800 U/min · K-Jetronic · Verdichtung 8,5 : 1 · Beschleunigung von 0–100 in 7,5 sec · Höchstgeschwindigkeit über 210 km/h · Mit Porsche-Langzeit-Garantie.

In 1975 the Carrera produced over 200 horsepower from 3-liter displacement with a relatively low compression of 8.5:1. The car no longer was quite as fast as the first Carrera, but it clearly had gained in sophistication.

PORSCHE CARRERA

In der 28-jährigen Geschichte des Hauses Porsche haben schon mehrere Modelle den Namen „Carrera" getragen, und fast immer waren es entweder reine Rennautos oder zumindest betont sportliche, auf hohe Leistung gebrachte Straßenfahrzeuge.

Beim heutigen Carrera 3.0 jedoch steht nicht mehr allein die Sportlichkeit an oberster Stelle, sondern gleichberechtigt der Komfort: Alles, was ein Porsche 911 zu bieten hat (und das ist eine Menge) ist beim Carrera noch verstärkt, verbessert, verfeinert, vervollkommnet. Der Motor ist noch bulliger und elastischer, der Geräuschpegel noch niedriger, die Ausstattung noch luxuriöser:

Das Carrera-Sportlenkrad hat nur 38 cm Durchmesser und einen dick gepolsterten Lederkranz.
Türgriffe und Fenstereinfassungen (beim Targa auch der Sicherheitsbügel) sind mattschwarz verchromt; die Scheinwerferringe und der Außenspiegel in der Wagenfarbe lackiert. Elektrische Fensterheber (auch beim Targa), Heckscheibenwischer, Scheinwerfer-Reinigungsanlage und automatische Heizungsregulierung sind selbstverständlich serienmäßig und machen das Fahren im Carrera noch angenehmer und sicherer.
Unter den verbreiterten hinteren Kotflügeln bringen Hochgeschwindigkeitsreifen der Dimension 215/60 VR 15 auf neuen Carrera-Rädern die 200 PS des 3-Liter-Motors in jeder Situation zuverlässig auf den Boden. Stabilisatoren vorn und hinten sorgen immer für maximalen Fahrbahnkontakt und – selbst in extrem gefahrenen Kurven – für minimale Aufbau-Neigung.

Den Komfort einer luxuriösen Reiselimousine und die Kraft eines reinrassigen Hochleistungssportwagens – der Carrera bietet beides.

Technische Daten

6-Zylinder-Boxermotor, luftgekühlt, hinten. Kraftübertragung über Doppelgelenkwelle auf die Hinterräder. 3,0 l Hubraum. 2993 ccm. 200 PS/147 kW bei 6000 U/min. K-Jetronic. Verdichtung 8,5:1. Beschleunigung von 0–100 in 6,3 sec. Höchstgeschwindigkeit über 230 km/h. Mit Porsche-Langzeit-Garantie.

PORSCHE CARRERA

In the 28-year history of the House of Porsche, several models have borne the name of "Carrera," and they almost always were pure racing cars or at least predominantly sporting road cars tuned to high performance.

In today's Carrera 3.0, though, sportiness alone is no longer at the top, but is equaled by comfort: everything that a Porsche 911 has to offer (and that's a lot) is even strengthened, improved, refined, and completed in the Carrera. The motor is even stronger and more flexible, the noise level is even lower, the furnishing even more luxurious.

The Carrera sport steering wheel has a diameter of only 38 cm and a thickly padded leather rim.

Door and window handles (and the Targa's roll bar too) are finished in matt black; the headlight rings and the outside mirror are painted the color of the car. Electric window controls (in the Targa too), rear window wiper, headlight-cleaning system and automatic heat regulation naturally are standard and make driving the Carrera even more pleasant and safer.

Under the widened rear fenders, high-speed tires of size 215/60 VR 15 on new Carrera wheels bring the 200 horsepower of the 3-liter motor to the ground reliably in every situation. Front and rear stabilizers always assure maximum road contact and—even in very fast curves—minimal body tilting.

The comfort of a luxurious traveling sedan and the power of a thoroughbred high-performance sports car—the Carrera offers both.

Technical Data

Six-cylinder boxer motor, air-cooled, rear-mounted—Power transmission via half-axles to the rear wheels—3.0-liter displacement—2993 cc—200 hp at 6000 rpm—K-Jetronic—8.5:1 compression—acceleration from 0 to 62 in 6.3 sec.—top speed over 143 mph—with Porsche's longtime guarantee.

The Turbo was presented in Paris in 1974; shown here in a contemporary catalog, it has been the top model of the 911 line since that time (even though its exact designation is 930 Turbo).

Along with the normal coupe version, there still was the Targa, but not with the turbo motor; meanwhile the bumpers had changed and now could absorb a weak blow.

52

1975

When the catalogs of the seventies and eighties were prepared, a great deal of emphasis was placed on the high artistic quality of the photos. Even small details of the 911 indicate its highly developed construction.

PORSCHE Practice

Every Porsche has an outside mirror electrically heatable and adjustable from the inside. Nobody can constantly keep an eye on the speedometer on roads with speed limits. On an empty superhighway it is a chore to have to give gas. Both are taken over by the "Tempostat": it holds any desired speed between 25 and 112 mph constantly without your foot touching the gas pedal. After a braking maneuver the previously registered desired speed can be recalled by your fingertip. The Tempostat remains fully functional during acceleration or gear changing. The headlight cleaning system likewise contributes to safety and comfort: water sprayed on the headlight lenses at 3.5 times normal pressure cleans off the light-devouring film of dirt and rinses it away (standard as of the Carrera).

The water filler cap of the 9-quart tank for the windshield and headlight cleaning system is under the same lid as the fuel filler cap. A "bib" protects the Porsche paint from scratches and scrapes. The rear-window wiper (standard as of the Carrera) provides an always-clear view to the rear. All Porsche coupes can, if desired, be fitted with an electrically operated steel sliding roof. An important contribution to comfort is the automatic heat regulation, for it makes unnecessary the frequent reaching for the heater lever during a trip. Independent of outside temperature, car speed and motor speed, a thermostat between the sun visors and one in the heating system assure a lasting interior temperature that one can choose on a scale with nine steps (standard as of the Carrera). When needed, the folded tire of the space-saving spare wheel can be pumped up with the new electric compressor.

op speed for the spare wheel: 100 mph.

The safety bumpers with their protector strips blend harmoniously and flowingly into the body lines. Yet in a collision at up to 5 mph nothing more is damaged than a quickly and cheaply replaced deformation element in the bumper attachment. The car survives the same collision completely unharmed when energy-absorbing dampers are installed in place of the deformable elements.

PORSCHE-Praktik

Jeder Porsche hat einen von innen elektrisch verstellbaren und beheizbaren Außenspiegel. Niemand kann auf Strecken mit Geschwindigkeitsbeschränkung ständig den Tachometer im Auge behalten. Und bei leerer Autobahn ist es lästig, überhaupt gasgeben zu müssen. Beides nimmt Ihnen der „Tempostat" ab: zwischen 40 und 180 km/h hält er jede gewünschte Geschwindigkeit konstant, ohne daß Ihr Fuß das Gaspedal berührt. Nach einem Bremsmanöver kann die zuvor eingespeicherte Wunschgeschwindigkeit durch einfachen Fingertip wieder abgerufen werden. Bei Beschleunigung oder Gangwechsel bleibt der Tempostat in voller Funktion.

Gleichermaßen der Sicherheit und der Bequemlichkeit dient die Scheinwerfer-Reinigungsanlage: Mit 3,5 atü auf die Scheinwerfergläser gesprühtes Wasser weicht den lichtschluckenden Schmutzfilm auf und spült ihn fort (ab Carrera serienmäßig).

Der Wassereinfüllstutzen des 8,5-Liter-Tanks für die Scheiben- und Scheinwerfer-Reinigung liegt unter derselben Klappe wie der Benzineinfüllstutzen. Ein „Lätzchen" schützt den Porsche-Lack vor Kratzern und Spritzern. Für immer freie Sicht nach hinten sorgt der (ab Carrera serienmäßige) Heckscheibenwischer. Auf Wunsch können alle Porsche-Coupés mit einem elektrischen Stahlschiebedach geliefert werden. Ein wesentlicher Komfort-Beitrag ist die automatische Heizungsregulierung, denn sie erspart während der Fahrt den häufigen Griff zum Heizungshebel. Unabhängig von Außentemperatur, Fahrgeschwindigkeit und Motordrehzahl sorgen ein Temperaturfühler zwischen den Sonnenblenden und einer im Heizungssystem für eine gleichbleibende Innenraum-Wärme, die man auf einer Sollwertskala mit neun Stufen vorwählen kann (ab Carrera serienmäßig).

Bei Bedarf wird der Faltreifen des platzsparenden Notrades mit dem neuen elektrischen Kompressor aufgepumpt. Höchstgeschwindigkeit für die Pannenbereifung: 160 km/h.

Die Sicherheits-Stoßstangen fügen sich mit ihrem Faltenbalg harmonisch und fließend in die Karosserielinie ein. Dennoch wird ein Aufprall bis 8 km/h nichts weiter beschädigt als ein schnell und billig austauschbares Deformations-Element in der Stoßstangen-Halterung. Völlig schadlos übersteht der Wagen den gleichen Aufprall, wenn anstelle der Deformations-Elemente energieabsorbierende Pralldämpfer montiert sind.

Offen fahren:
PORSCHE TARGA:

Offen fahren: das ist die Urform des Fahrens – und nach wie vor die schönste.

Die klassischen Roadster und Speedster – für viele der Inbegriff des Sportwagens überhaupt – haben nur einen Haken: Sie machen zwar sehr viel Spaß, aber wenn's Ernst wird, werden sie kritisch: Kaum einer von ihnen erfüllt die vom Gesetzgeber aufgestellten Sicherheitsanforderungen bei Crash- und Überschlagstests. Diese Entwicklung vorausahnend, hat Porsche schon vor Jahren ein völlig neues Cabrio-Konzept geschaffen – den Targa. In dieser Version sind der 911 und der Carrera lieferbar.

Sein integrierter Überrollbügel verleiht dem Targa beim Aufprallen und Abrollen genau die gleichen Eigenschaften wie beim Coupé hinsichtlich Sicherheit der Fahrgastzelle und passivem Unfallschutz der Insassen.

Mit wenigen Handgriffen ist das stabile Faltdach abgenommen, platzsparend zusammengelegt und im Auto verstaut – jetzt steht Ihnen der Himmel offen und Sie genießen alle Vorteile eines Cabrios, brauchen aber keinen einzigen seiner Nachteile in Kauf zu nehmen: Das Targa-Dach ist wartungsfrei, es schließt geräuschlos, zugfrei, wind- und wasserdicht. Der Sicherheitsbügel besteht aus rostfreiem Stahl, beim Carrera Targa mattschwarz eloxiert.

In beiden Targa-Modellen ist die Heckscheibe getönt, zweistufig beheizbar und mit Wischer ausgerüstet.

Keine Angst vor Langfingern, wenn Sie offen parken: Selbstverständlich ist die Entriegelung des Kofferraumdeckels abschließbar.

Open driving:
PORSCHE TARGA

Open driving is the original form of driving—and now as then the nicest.

The classic Roadster and Speedster—for many the essence of sports cars—have only one problem: they are a lot of fun, but when things get serious they become critical. Scarcely one of them fulfills the legal safety regulations in crash and turnover tests. Anticipating this development from the start, Porsche created a new convertible concept years ago: the Targa. The 911 and the Carrera are available in this version.

Its integrated roll bar gives the Targa exactly the same crashing and rolling characteristics as a coupe in terms of passenger safety and passive protection of the occupants.

The stable folding roof can be removed with a few easy moves, folded up and stowed in the car, taking up little space. Now the skies are open and you enjoy all the advantages of a convertible but don't need to accept a single one of its disadvantages: the Targa roof is service-free, closes silently, is draft-free, air- and watertight. The roll bar is made of stainless steel, and finished in matt black in the Carrera Targa.

In both Targa models the rear window is tinted, heated at two levels and equipped with a wiper.

Don't worry about thieves when you park it open: naturally the luggage-space release can be locked.

The operation of the Targa roof in practice turns out to be nowhere near as playful as these photos are meant to show. In the new Targa the rear panel can no longer be folded up.

Motor

Alle Porsche der 911-Baureihe haben robuste, auf hohe Dauerleistungen ausgelegte Sechszylinder-Boxer-Motoren mit je drei Zylindern rechts und links vom Kurbelgehäuse. Diese Anordnung ergibt kompakte Abmessungen, vor allem die im Sportwagen erforderliche niedrige Bauhöhe.

Die hängenden Ventile sind V-förmig angeordnet und werden durch je eine obenliegende Nockenwelle pro Zylinderreihe gesteuert. Die geschmiedete Kurbelwelle ist sorgfältig ausgewuchtet und läuft in acht Lagern.

Als einer der wenigen Fahrzeughersteller leistet sich Porsche auch bei seinen Serien-Autos die sonst nur im Rennwagenbau verwendete Trockensumpfschmierung. Sie überlistet die Fliehkraft und versorgt auch bei extrem schneller Kurvenfahrt alle Schmierstellen mit gereinigtem und gekühltem Öl in der richtigen Menge.

Alle Porsche haben Startautomatic.

Die Gemischaufbereitung erfolgt in allen Porsche-Motoren durch eine kontinuierliche Benzineinspritzung: die K-Jetronic.

Die kontaktlos gesteuerte und damit wartungsfreie Zündanlage wurde für den Motorsport entwickelt und ist hier in die Serie übernommen worden.

Eine Stunde lang muß jeder Porsche-Motor auf dem Prüfstand beweisen, daß er unter allen Be-

dingungen einwandfrei arbeitet und alle Ansprüche in punkto Dichtheit, Leistung, Verbrauch, Geräusch und Abgas voll erfüllt.

Das Besondere am Turbo-Motor ist natürlich der Turbolader. Er besteht aus einem Turbinen- und einem Verdichterrad, die auf einer gemeinsamen Welle befestigt sind. Das Turbinenrad wird von den Auspuffgasen des Motors angetrieben und bis auf Drehzahlen von 90000 U/min gebracht. Mit der gleichen Geschwindigkeit dreht sich auch das Verdichterrad. Es saugt über den Luftfilter, den Gemischregler und die Saugleitung Luft an, verdichtet sie bis auf 0,8 atü und führt sie über Druckleitung, Drosselklappe und Ansaugverteiler den Zylindern zu. Die Gemischbildung erfolgt in einer gegenüber den Saugmotoren vergrößerten K-Jetronic-Anlage. Diese wurde zusätzlich mit einem Startmagnet versehen, der bei heißem Motor und eventuellem Ausdampfen der Einspritzleitungen kurzzeitig die Einspritzmenge erhöht und somit einen sicheren Heißstart gewährleistet.

Motor

All 911-series Porsches have robust six-cylinder motors, with three cylinders each right and left of the crankcase, built for lasting high performance. This arrangement gives compact dimensions, especially the low height necessary in sports cars.

The dropped valves are set in V-form and are activated by one overhead camshaft per cylinder bank. The forged crankshaft is balanced carefully and runs in eight bearings. Porsche is one of few automobile manufacturers to utilize dry-sump lubrication—otherwise used only in racing cars—in its production cars. It outsmarts centrifugal force and assures the correct amount of cleaned and cooled oil to all lubrication points even during extremely fast cornering. All Porsches have automatic starting.

The mixture of fuel takes place in all Porsche motors by means of continual K-Jetronic fuel injection.

For an hour every Porsche motor must prove on the test bench that it works faultlessly

under all conditions and fully fulfills all requirements in terms of steadiness, performance, consumption, sound and exhaust.

The special feature of the Turbo motor is naturally the turbocharger. It consists of a turbine and a compression wheel attached to a common shaft. The turbine is run by the motor's exhaust gases and reaches turning speeds up to 90,000 rpm. The compressor wheel also turns at the same speed. It sucks in air via the air filter, mixing regulator and intake pipes, compresses it to 0.8 atu, and sends it to the cylinders via the pressure pipes, throttle valve and injection dividers. Mixing takes place in an enlarged K-Jetronic unit opposite the intake motors. This also is equipped with a starting magnet, which quickly increases the injected amount when the motor is hot and evaporation may take place in the induction pipes, thus assuring sure hot-engine starting.

The ignition system, having no contact points and therefore service-free, was developed for motor sport and has been put into series production here.

Turbo Status

Elegance dominates the Turbo cockpit: In front of you is a plaque engraved with your name, behind you 260 horsepower. Thus Turbo owners travel belted into seats of the finest leather combined with costly woolen fabrics, and nothing disturbs them as they enjoy stereo from four speakers.

Naturally, the radio also includes a station selector and an automatic motorized antenna.

The windows, tinted all around, guarantee pleasant coolness in summer and an ever-clear view in winter, for the windshield also is electrically heated, as is the rear window in two stages. Electric window controls are standard, as are the headlight-cleaning system, the rear-window wiper, the nonstep wiper speed switch, the fog lights and the perfect heat comfort by means of automatic maintenance of the chosen interior temperature.

Starting and accelerating is breathtaking, as the pressure on your back grows stronger; and comforting, as the Turbo's gauges inform the driver of the machine's good health. Five instrument dials give, to fractions of a second, information about fuel supply, oil level, oil temperature, oil pressure, fuel pressure, engine speed, road speed, clock time and even more.

The suspension, with its Turbo-specific qualities and braking-power intensification, shows that a fast car need not give a hard ride. The ultra-low-pressure tires on 16-inch wheels contribute much to this.

Its height-to-width ratio is 50 to 100—in racing-car technology with sedan comfort.

Technical Data

Six-cylinder boxer motor, air-cooled, rear-mounted. Power transmission via half-axles to the rear wheels. 3.0-liter displacement, 2993 cc. 260 hp at 5500 rpm. Maximum torque 35 mkp at 4000 rpm. K-Jetronic with turbocharger. 6.5:1 compression. Acceleration from 0 to 62 mph in 5.5 seconds. Top speed over 155 mph. One-year guarantee without mileage restriction, six year no-rust guarantee.

Open driving: PORSCHE TARGA:

Open driving is the original form of driving—and now as then the nicest.

The classic Roadster and Speedster—for many the essence of sports cars—have just one problem: they are a lot of fun, but when things get serious they become critical. Scarcely one of them fulfills the legal safety regulations in crash and turnover tests. Anticipating this development from the start, Porsche created a new convertible concept years ago: the Targa. The 911 and Carrera are available in this version.

Its integrated roll bar gives the Targa exactly the same crashing and rolling characteristics as a coupe in terms of passenger safety and passive protection of the occupants.

The stable folding roof can be removed with a few simple moves, folded up and stowed in the car. Now the skies are open and you enjoy all the advantages of a convertible but don't need to accept a single one of the disadvantages: the Targa roof is service-free, closes silently, is draft-free, air- and watertight. The roll bar consists of stainless steel, and finished in matt black in the Carrera Targa.

In both Targa models the rear window is tinted, heated at two levels and equipped with a wiper.

Don't worry about thieves when you park open: naturally the luggage-space release can be locked.

Turbo-Status

Im Turbo-Cockpit dominiert Eleganz: Vor sich eine Plakette mit ihrem eingravierten Namen, hinter sich 260 PS – so reisen Turbo-Eigner entspannt in Sesseln aus feinstem Leder, mit wertvollen Wollstoffen kombiniert, und nichts stört sie beim Stereo-Genuß aus vier Lautsprechern.

Selbstverständlich verfügt das Radio auch über einen Sendersuchlauf und eine automatische Motor-Antenne.

Die rundum getönte Verglasung garantiert im Sommer angenehme Kühle und im Winter stets klare Sicht, denn auch die Frontscheibe ist elektrisch beheizbar, die Heckscheibe sogar in zwei Stufen. Elektrische Fensterheber sind ebenso serienmäßig wie die Scheinwerfer-Reinigungs-anlage, der Heckscheibenwischer, der stufen-los einstellbare Wisch-Intervallschalter, die Nebelscheinwerfer und der perfekte Heizkom-fort, bei dem eine automatische Regulierung die vorgewählte Innenraum-Temperatur stabilisiert.

Start und Beschleunigung: Atemberaubend, wie der Druck im Rücken immer stärker wird; und beruhigend, wie die Turbo-Armaturen den Fah-rer über das Wohlbefinden der Maschine infor-mieren: Fünf Rundinstrumente geben in Sekun-denbruchteilen Auskunft über Kraftstoffreserve, Ölstand, Öltemperatur, Öldruck, Ladedruck, Motordrehzahl, Fahrgeschwindigkeit, Uhrzeit und etliches mehr.

Das Fahrwerk mit Turbo-spezifischer Kinematik und Bremskraftverstärker beweist, daß ein schnelles Auto nicht hart sein muß. Dazu tragen die Ultra-Niederquerschnittsreifen auf 16 Zoll-Rädern maßgeblich bei.

Ihr Höhen-zu-Breiten-Verhältnis: 50 zu 100. Das ist Rennwagen-Technik mit Limousinen-Komfort.

Technische Daten

6-Zylinder-Boxermotor, luftgekühlt, hinten. Kraft-übertragung über Doppelgelenkwelle auf die Hinterräder. 3,0 l Hubraum. 2993 ccm. 260 PS / 191 kW bei 5500 U/min. Max. Drehmoment 35 mkp bei 4000 U/min. K-Jetronic mit Turbo-auflader. Verdichtung 6,5:1. Beschleunigung von 0–100 in 5,5 sec. Höchstgeschwindigkeit über 250 km/h. 1 Jahr Garantie ohne Kilometer-beschränkung. 6 Jahre Langzeit-Garantie gegen Rost.

Offen fahren: PORSCHE TARGA:

Offen fahren: das ist die Urform des Fahrens – und nach wie vor die schönste.

Die klassischen Roadster und Speedster – für viele der Inbegriff des Sportwagens überhaupt – haben nur einen Haken: Sie machen zwar sehr viel Spaß, aber wenn's Ernst wird, werden sie kritisch: Kaum einer von ihnen erfüllt die vom Gesetzgeber aufgestellten Sicherheitsanforde-rungen bei Crash- und Überschlagstests. Diese Entwicklung vorausahnend, hat Porsche schon vor Jahren ein völlig neues Cabrio-Konzept geschaffen – den Targa. In dieser Version sind der 911 und der Carrera lieferbar.

Sein integrierter Überrollbügel verleiht dem Targa beim Aufprallen und Abrollen genau die gleichen Eigenschaften wie beim Coupé hinsichtlich Sicherheit der Fahrgastzelle und passivem Unfall-schutz der Insassen.

Mit wenigen Handgriffen ist das stabile Faltdach abgenommen, platzsparend zusammengelegt und im Auto verstaut – jetzt steht Ihnen der Himmel offen und sie genießen alle Vorteile eines Cabrios, brauchen aber keinen einzigen seiner Nachteile in Kauf zu nehmen: Das Targa-Dach ist wartungsfrei, es schließt geräuschlos, zugfrei, wind- und wasserdicht. Der Sicherheits-bügel besteht aus rostfreiem Stahl, beim Carrera Targa mattschwarz eloxiert.

In beiden Targa-Modellen ist die Heckscheibe getönt, zweistufig beheizbar und mit Wischer ausgerüstet.

Keine Angst vor Langfingern, wenn Sie offen parken: Selbstverständlich ist die Entriegelung des Kofferraumdeckels abschließbar.

View of the
Porsche
factory and
test track in
Stuttgart-Zuffen-
hausen.

57

With the 911 the emphasis is not placed on its racing-car development alone, but more on pleasurable driving in close contact with the environment, always with the awareness of motoring superiority.

PORSCHE 911

Wer vom Porsche spricht, meint in aller Regel den 911, unser Basis-Modell, den »Porsche an sich«.

Einen 911 gab es bereits 1964 – und er sah damals kaum anders aus als heute. Er war nicht nur fast ebenso schön – er war auch fast ebenso schnell: 210 km/h.

Was also haben wir seither getan?

Elf Jahre Modellkonstanz, das heißt elf Jahre Feinarbeit am Detail: kaum zu sehen, aber sofort zu spüren. Eine Vergleichsfahrt von nur wenigen Minuten Dauer würde Ihnen den entscheidenden Unterschied deutlich machen. Im Porsche von heute erscheint Ihnen das gleiche Tempo nur halb so schnell – und halb so anstrengend. Die gleiche Leistung fällt bei Drehzahlen an, die um ein Drittel niedriger liegen. Das höhere Drehmoment erlaubt längere Getriebeübersetzungen und macht den Motor elastisch. Man muß viel seltener schalten. Und – es ist wesentlich leiser geworden im Porsche.

Doch ein paar Minuten reichen nicht aus, um alle Ergebnisse von elf Jahren Arbeit zu erfühlen und zu erfahren: Sie rollen gut 600 Kilometer bis zum nächsten Tank-Stop an einer »Normal«-Zapfsäule. 20 000 Kilometer lang braucht Ihr Porsche keinen Ölwechsel und keine Inspektion. Und die einjährige Garantie gilt auch dann, wenn Sie in dieser Zeit 50 000 Kilometer oder mehr zurücklegen.

Ja – Porsche-Fahren ist heute wirtschaftlicher als jemals zuvor, denn der Porsche geht schonend um mit dem Material, mit dem Treibstoff, mit seinen Insassen und mit seiner Umwelt. Er ist »feiner« geworden – aber robust geblieben. Er hat viel an Komfort gewonnen – aber nichts von seiner Sportlichkeit verloren.

Er ist – wie eh und je – exclusiv. Und dabei so alltagstauglich und verkehrsgerecht wie kein anderer seiner Klasse. Autokenner in aller Welt behaupten, daß er zeitlos sei. Wir meinen, daß er zeitgemäß ist. Und wir kümmern uns darum, daß er seiner Zeit immer ein paar gute Ideen voraus ist.

PORSCHE 911

Anyone who talks about the Porsche generally means the 911, our basic model, the "Porsche in and of itself."

There already was a 911 in 1964—and at that time it scarcely looked different from today. It not only almost was as beautiful— it also almost was as fast: 130 mph.

So what have we done since then?

Eleven years of the same model means eleven years of fine work in detail: scarcely visible, but felt at once. A comparison drive of only a few minutes would make the essential difference clear to you. In today's Porsche the same speed seems only half as fast—and half as demanding. The same performance is achieved at engine speeds that are one-third slower. The higher torque allows longer gear times and makes the motor flexible. You need to shift much less often—and it has become much easier in the Porsche.

But a few minutes are not enough to give all the results of eleven years a chance to work and to experience them. You drive a good 370 miles to the next stop at a "regular" pump. For 12,500 miles your Porsche needs no oil change or check-up. The one-year guarantee applies even if you cover 31,000 miles or more in that time.

Yes—Porsche driving is more economical today than ever before, for the Porsche is kind to its materials, fuel, passengers and environment. It has become more "refined"—but remained robust. It has gained much in comfort—but lost none of its sportiness.

It is—as always—exclusive, and yet as useful and practical in everyday traffic as no other car in its class. Car experts all over the world maintain that it is timeless. We think it is timely. And we make sure it is always a few good ideas ahead of its time.

Suspension

Safety, sportiness and riding comfort—those are the requirements of the Porsche suspension, built for 168 mph. Its essential elements are the same in all models: the front wheels are mounted independently and led by transverse links along with shock absorbers, and sprung on torsion bars. A front stabilizer—and a rear one, too, in the Carrera and Turbo—decrease lateral tilting. The rear wheels are mounted independently on light metal diagonal links. A transverse spring takes care of each wheel. Road jolts and spring bouncing are eliminated in the shock absorbers by means of oil compression (also gas pressure in the Turbo). In the Carrera and Turbo, high-speed front and rear tires of different widths on light metal wheels provide the best possible contact with the road, give extreme cornering safety and perfect road attitude. The dual-circuit braking system with four internally cooled, fadeproof disc brakes brings the Porsche from 62 to 0 mph on a dry road in 3.2 seconds. The precise, direct and light rack-and-pinion steering has a three-section safety steering column that cannot push into the interior of the car in an accident.

Fahrwerk

Sicherheit, Sportlichkeit und Fahrkomfort – das sind die Anforderungen an das für 270 km/h ausgelegte Porsche-Fahrwerk. Seine wesentlichen Elemente sind bei allen Modellen gleich: Die Vorderräder sind einzeln aufgehängt und werden von Querlenkern zusammen mit Dämpferbeinen geführt und von Drehstäben gefedert. Stabilisatoren vorn – und bei Carrera und Turbo auch hinten – verringern die Seitenneigung. Die Hinterräder sind einzeln an Leichtmetall-Schräglenkern aufgehängt. Ein querliegender Federstab pro Rad übernimmt die Federung. Fahrbahnstöße und Federschwingungen werden durch Ölverdrängung im Stoßdämpfer (beim Turbo zusätzlich mit Gasdruck) abgebaut. Bei Carrera und Turbo sorgen vorn und hinten unterschiedlich breite Hochgeschwindigkeitsreifen auf Leichtmetallfelgen für bestmöglichen Kontakt zur Fahrbahn, für extreme Kurvensicherheit und für perfekte Straßenlage. Die Zweikreis-Bremsanlage mit vier innenbelüfteten, fadingfesten Scheibenbremsen verzögert den Porsche auf trockener Fahrbahn in 3,2 Sekunden von 100 auf 0 km/h. Die präzise, direkte und leichtgängige Zahnstangenlenkung hat eine dreigeteilte Sicherheits-Lenksäule, die sich bei einem Aufprall nicht ins Wageninnere schieben kann.

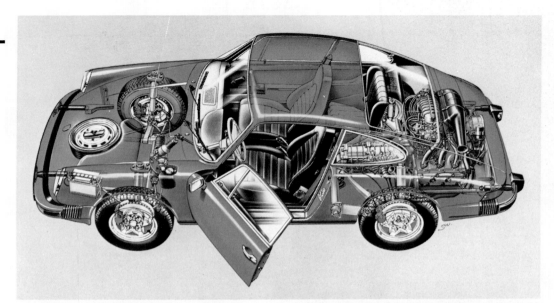

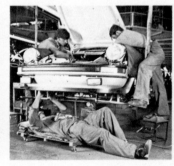

Such an "X-ray" as this catalog portrays lets one see the individual organs of the Porsche 911 clearly and shows the resulting utilization of space, particularly in the front end of the car.

Carrera – ein reinrassiger Hochleistungssportwagen mit der Ausstattung einer luxuriösen Reiselimousine: Elektrische Fensterheber (im Coupé) und von innen elektrisch verstellbarer und beheizbarer Außenspiegel sind serienmäßig. Türgriffe und Fenstereinfassungen sind matt schwarz verchromt, die Scheinwerferringe und der Außenspiegel in der Wagenfarbe lackiert. Sitze und Innenausstattung wahlweise in Stoff oder Kunstleder lieferbar. Der Teppich ist Hochflor. Das Sportlenkrad hat nur 38 cm Durchmesser und einen dick gepolsterten Lederkranz. Der Scheibenwischer hat 3 Geschwindigkeiten und zusätzlich einen Intervallschalter. Unter den verbreiterten hinteren Kotflügeln bringen Hochgeschwindigkeitsreifen der Dimension 215/60 VR 15 die 200 PS des 3-Liter-Carrera-Motors in jeder Situation sicher auf den Boden. Vorn rollt der Carrera auf Reifen der Größe 185/70 VR 15. Die Felgen dazu sind 6 J x 15 und 7 J x 15.

Carrera—a thoroughbred, high-performance sports car equipped like a luxurious sedan: electric window controls (in the coupe) and an outside mirror electrically adjustable and heatable from within are standard. Door and window handles are finished in matt black, the headlight rings and outside mirrors are painted the color of the car. Seats and interior decor are in your choice of fabric or leatherette. The carpeting is high-pile. The sport-type steering wheel has a diameter of only centimeters and a thickly padded leather ring. The windshield wipers have three speeds and an interval control too. Under the widened rear fenders, high-speed 215/60 VR 15 tires put the 200 horsepower of the 3-liter Carrera on the road surely in any situation. The Porsche's front end rolls on 185/70 VR 15 tires. The wheels are 6 J x 15 and 7 J x 15.

Im Porsche bilden Sitz und Kopfstützen eine organische Einheit. Sie garantieren auf Langstrecken ein ermüdungsfreies Fahren und geben auch in kritischen Situationen – in Kombination mit dem Dreipunkt-Sicherheitsgurt – Fahrer und Beifahrer sicheren Halt.

In the Porsche the seat and headrest are one organic unit. They guarantee fatigue-free driving on a long trip and give the driver and passenger sure support in critical situations—along with the three-point seat belt.

Die Rücksitze bieten auf kurzen Strecken zwei Erwachsenen und auf langen Reisen zwei Kindern ausreichenden Platz. Heruntergeklappt nehmen sie 230 Liter Gepäck auf und halten es rutschsicher fest. Durch die vielen Ablagemöglichkeiten liegt im Porsche nichts lose herum, was bei einer Notbremsung als »Geschoß« wirken könnte. Was nicht in den geräumigen Handschuhkasten paßt, findet in den vier Türablagen sicher Platz.

The rear seats offer adequate seating for two adults on short trips and for two children on long trips. Folded down, they carry 60 gallons of luggage and secure it from sliding. What with the many stowage facilities, nothing lies around loose in a Porsche that could become a "projectile" under emergency braking. Whatever won't fit in the glove compartment finds a safe place in the four door pockets.

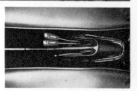

Safety first – im Porsche dominiert die Sicherheit: Alle Armaturen, Schalter und Knöpfe sind weich gepolstert und so angeordnet, daß sie im Ernstfall keine Verletzungsgefahr darstellen. Fünf große Anzeigeinstrumente liefern blendfrei alle notwendigen Informationen, ohne den Blick des Fahrers länger als für Sekundenbruchteile von der Fahrbahn abzulenken.

Safety first—safety dominates in the Porsche. All gauges, switches and buttons are upholstered softly and arranged so that they cause no danger of injury in a serious situation. Five large instrument dials give all the necessary information without glare, without taking the driver's eyes off the road for more than a fraction of a second.

The PORSCHE Exhaust-Driven Turbocharger

The motor sucks fresh air in via the air filter (1), mixing regulator (2) and intake pipes (4), which is conducted through the compressor (5) of the turbocharger into the compression pipes (6) and throttle control housing (7) to the air divider (8) and thus into the motor. The motor's exhaust is led through the exhaust collector pipes (10) over the turbine (13) of the charger to the air via the muffler (14) into the air. The turbine (13) is driven by the exhaust stream, in turn driving the compressor (5), which conducts the fresh air to the motor under higher pressure. A bypass valve (12) set in the exhaust piping regulates the pressure of the compressor (5), in that higher pressure causes a control mechanism (15) to open the bypass valve (12), and the exhaust stream goes through the bypass pipe (11) around the turbine (13) and directly to the muffler (14). To maintain charger speed, for example when shifting or accelerating, there is a connection with a blowoff valve (3) between the intake pipes (4) and the compression pipes (6). The blowoff valve (3) is activated by a cutting control mechanism (17) in which, when the throttle valve is closed, the blowoff valve (3) is opened by lower pressure, so that the fresh air stream circulates around the compressor (5) and the charger speed is maintained.

A front spoiler extending from the Carrera's front skirt and a rear spoiler reduce the lift forces of the Turbo by about 100 percent and thus improve the tracking, steering, cornering and lateral attitude relatively more as the speed increases. A further noteworthy mark of the body is the widening of the front and rear fenders. It corresponds generally to the form of the racing Carrera (RSR) of 1973 and the RS 74, and are leading to a future sanction for competition.

Technical data:
3.0-liter displacement, 260 hp, 191.3 kW at 5500 rpm, maximum torque 35 mkp at 4000 rpm, acceleration from 0 to 62 mph in 5.5 seconds, top speed over 155 mph.
Standard equipment:
Coupe; 4-speed transmission; forged light metal wheels; front 7 J x 15, rear 8 J x 15, with 205/50 VR 15 and 225/50 VR 15 tires; front and rear stabilizers; gas-pressure shock absorbers; seats and interior decor in combination of leather and plaid; high-pile carpeting; adhesive "Turbo" label on the left rear seat back; all chrome trim in matt black; headlight rings and outside mirror in the car's color; front and rear spoiler; leather steering wheel; electric window controls; outside mirror adjusted and warmed electrically from inside; windshield wiper interval switch; automatic heat regulation; headlight cleaning system; lighted door/ignition key; tinted glass all around; rear window with two-stage defroster; windshield defroster; rear window wiper; Blaupunkt Cologne stereo radio with tuning; electric antenna and four speakers; fog lights; body color metallic or any desired special or production color. A choice of additional equipment: electric sliding roof, air conditioning, fog light covers.

Die PORSCHE-Abgas-Turbo-Aufladung

Der Motor saugt über den Luftfilter (1), den Gemischregler (2) über die Saugleitung (4) Frischluft an, die über den Verdichter (5) des Laders in die Druckleitung (6), das Drosselklappengehäuse (7), zu dem Luftverteiler (8) und somit dem Motor zugeführt wird. Der Abgasstrom des Motors wird durch eine Abgassammelleitung (10) über die Turbine (13) des Laders, über den Schalldämpfer (14) ins Freie geleitet. Durch den Abgasstrom wird die Turbine (13) angetrieben, die wiederum den Verdichter (5) antreibt, der die Frischluft unter Überdruck dem Motor zuführt. Ein in die Abgasleitung (10) eingesetztes Bypassventil (12) regelt den Ladedruck des Verdichters (5), indem über eine Steuerleitung (15) durch den Ladeüberdruck das Bypassventil (12) geöffnet wird und der Abgasstrom über die Bypassleitung (11) unter Umgehung der Turbine (13) direkt zum Schalldämpfer (14) gelangt. Zur Aufrechterhaltung der Laderdrehzahl, z.B. bei Schiebebetrieb des Fahrzeuges, bzw. um ein schnelles Ansprechen des Motores beim Beschleunigen zu erhalten, ist zwischen der Saugleitung (4) und der Druckleitung (6) eine Verbindungsleitung mit einem Abblaseventil (3) angeordnet. Das Abblaseventil (3) wird über eine weitere Steuerleitung (17) betätigt, in welcher bei geschlossener Drosselklappe durch Unterdruck das Abblaseventil (3) geöffnet wird, so daß ein Kreislauf des Frischluftstromes um den Verdichter (5) entsteht, wodurch die Laderdrehzahl aufrecht erhalten bleibt.

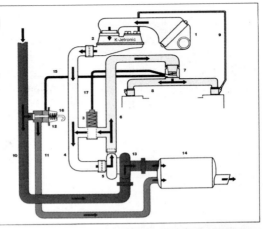

Ein von der Carrera-Bugschürze abgeleiteter Bugspoiler und ein Heckspoiler reduzieren beim Turbo die Auftriebskräfte um nahezu 100% und verbessern so das Brems-, Lenk-, Kurven- und Seitenwindverhalten relativ mehr, je höher die Fahrgeschwindigkeiten liegen. Ein weiteres hervorstehendes Karosseriemerkmal sind die großen Kotflügelverbreiterungen vorn und hinten. Sie entsprechen in etwa der Form denen des Renn-Carrera (RSR) 1973 und der RS 74 und berücksichtigen schon jetzt eine künftige Homologation für den Wettbewerb.

Technische Daten:
3,0 l Hubraum, 260 PS, 191,3 kW bei 5500 U/min, max. Drehmoment 35 mkp bei 4000 U/min, Beschleunigung 0 – 100 km/h in 5,5 Sekunden, Höchstgeschwindigkeit über 250 km/h.
Serien-Ausstattung:
Coupé, 4-Gang-Getriebe, Leichtmetallräder, geschmiedet, vorn 7 J x 15, hinten 8 J x 15 mit Reifen 205/50 VR 15 und 225/50 VR 15, Stabilisator vorn und hinten, Gasdruck-Stoßdämpfer, Sitze und Innenausstattung in Leder-Schottenstoffkombination, Teppich in Hochflor, gestickter »Turbo«-Schriftzug auf der linken Rücksitzlehne, sämtliche Zierleisten in Mattschwarz, Scheinwerferringe und Außenspiegel in Wagenfarbe, Front- und Heckspoiler, Leder-Sportlenkrad, elektrische Fensterheber, von innen elektrisch verstellbarer und beheizbarer Außenspiegel, Scheibenwischer-Intervallschalter, automatische Heizungsregulierung, Scheinwerfer-Reinigungsanlage, beleuchteter Tür-/Zündschlüssel, getönte Rundumverglasung, zweistufig beheizbare Heckscheibe, beheizbare Frontscheibe, Heckscheibenwischer, Stereo-Radio Blaupunkt Köln mit Suchlauf, elektrischer Antenne und 4 Lautsprechern, Nebelscheinwerfer, Wagenfarbe metallic oder jede beliebige Sonder- oder Serienlackierung.
Eine Auswahl an Mehrausstattung:
elektrisches Schiebedach
Klimaanlage
Nebelschlußleuchte

Here the operation of the powerful turbo aggregate is explained. At that time, in the mid-seventies, it already produced 260 horsepower and moved the car from zero to 62 mph in 5.5 seconds, beyond all competition.

61

Sicherheit im Porsche 911 SC:
Aktiv- und Passiv-Reserven

Die Porsche-Sicherheitsstoßstangen an Bug und Heck fügen sich mit ihrer Faltenbalg-Abdeckung harmonisch und fließend in die Karosserielinie ein.

Auf zweierlei Weise stützen sie sich an den Fahrzeug-Längsträgern ab: entweder durch jeweils zwei leicht austauschbare Deformationselemente in der Stoßstangen-Halterung oder – gegen Mehrpreis – durch energieabsorbierende hydraulische Pralldämpfer, die nach Kollisionen bis 8 km/h wieder in ihre ursprüngliche Lage zurückkehren. Selbstverständlich ist die Windschutzscheibe aus Verbundglas. Die zweifach abgewinkelte Sicherheitslenksäule kann sich bei

einem Zusammenstoß nicht ins Wageninnere schieben. Der Tank liegt in einer verformungsgeschützten Zone, und das gesamte Kraftstoffleitungssystem ist so konstruiert, daß auch nach einem 50 km/h-Crash und kopfstehendem Fahrzeug kein Tropfen Benzin ausläuft. Die Fahrgastzelle von Coupé und Targa übersteht Aufprall-Unfälle und mehrfache Überschläge ohne nennenswerte Deformation; die Türen bleiben sicher geschlossen und lassen sich anschließend anstandslos öffnen. Alle Armaturen, Schalter und Knöpfe sind weich gepolstert und so angeordnet, daß sie im Ernstfall keine Verletzungsgefahr darstellen.

**Safety in the Porsche 911 SC
Active and Passive Reserves**

The Porsche front and rear safety bumpers blend harmoniously and smoothly into the body lines, along with their accordion-pleated protectors.

They are connected to the longitudinal chassis members in two ways: either by two easily replaceable deformable structures in the bumper attachments, or—at extra cost—by energy-absorbing hydraulic collision dampers, which spring back to their original place after a collision of up to 5 mph. Naturally the windshield is made of safety glass. The two-jointed safety steering column will not push into the interior of the car in a collision. The tank is in a nondeformable area, and the entire fuel system is constructed so that the car can have a 31-mph collision and turn over without losing a single drop of fuel. The passenger compartments of the coupe and Targa withstand collisions and repeated rolling without noteworthy deforming; the doors stay closed securely and can be opened without trouble afterward. All gauges, switches and buttons are padded softly and arranged so as to cause no danger of injury in a serious situation.

Left: In 1978 the 911 SC had replaced the 911 and Carrera. Initially it had a respectable 180 horsepower and was available in coupe or Targa form.

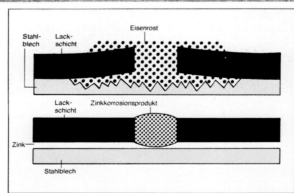

Sheet steel   Paint layer   Iron rust

       Paint layer   Zinc corrosion product

Zinc

       Sheet steel

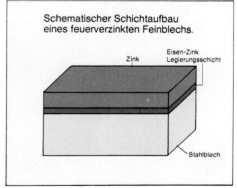

Schematic layered construction
of fire-zinced fine sheet steel

Zinc   Iron-zinc alloy layer

         Sheet steel

At this time the body was made of fire-zinced pieces of sheet metal, which protected it safely from rust along with the quality finish. Thus Porsche could give the 911 a six-year rust-free guarantee.

Ein geräumiges Handschuhfach, zwei offene und zwei geschlossene Tür-Ablagen sowie zwei Kartentaschen sorgen dafür, daß im Porsche nichts lose herumliegt, was bei einem scharfen Bremsvorgang als gefährliches »Geschoß« umherfliegen könnte. Mit diesen Eigenschaften zum Insassenschutz liegt der Porsche weit über den vom Gesetzgeber geforderten Werten. Doch viel wichtiger als die streng reglementierte passive Sicherheit erscheint uns – gerade bei einem Sportwagen – die aktive: Sie umfaßt alles, was dem Fahrer ermöglicht, kritische Situationen gefahrlos zu meistern, es gar nicht erst zum Unfall kom-

men zu lassen und bei Bedarf auch die Flucht nach vorn anzutreten. Dafür ist der Porsche mit seiner spontan verfügbaren Leistungs-Reserve ebenso gut gerüstet wie mit seinem tiefliegenden Schwerpunkt oder seiner enormen Querbeschleunigung.

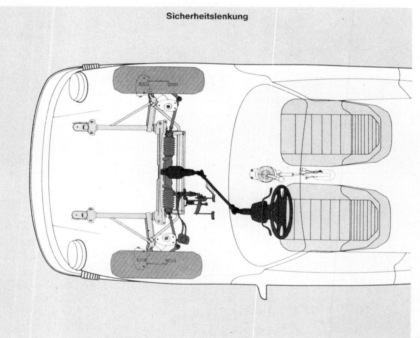

Sicherheitslenkung

safety steering

A roomy glove compartment, two open and two closed door pockets and two map pockets make sure that nothing lies around loose in a Porsche to fly around as a dangerous ''projectile'' under heavy braking. With these passenger safety features the Porsche is far above the legal standards. But much more important than the strictly regulated passive safety measures are—it seems to us— the active ones: This includes everything that makes it possible for the driver to master critical situations without danger, avoid accidents and, if necessary, to move ahead too. For that the Porsche, with its spontaneous performance reserve, is as well equipped as with its low center of gravity or its enormous acceleration.

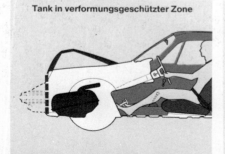

Tank in verformungsgeschützter Zone

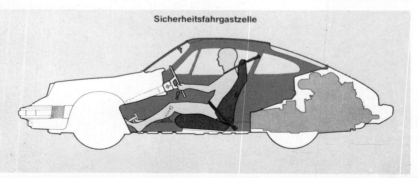

Sicherheitsfahrgastzelle

tank in non-deformable area

safety passenger compartment

The Suspension
With its standard Porsche synchronized five-speed transmission, the 911 SC always can be operated in the optimal engine speed area. To save weight the gearbox is made of very light silumin. The differential is identical to those of the top-line Porsche Turbo and 928; if desired, it can be provided with 40 percent locking effect.

Front Suspension

Rear Suspension

The drive of the rear wheels takes place via double-joint half-axles. An easily moving clutch with its standard clutch assistance requires only a little pedal pressure and effects a very comfortable power transmission when clutching.
All of these facts show clearly: "longtime quality" at Porsche is not limited to a six-year guarantee against the rusting of stressed body parts. There actually is much more to it: a constructive overdimensioning of all construction units in choice of materials, in durability and low demands in service and care.
These qualities assure and maintain the optical and technical new value of every Porsche for many years and make used Porsches just as desirable as they are risk-free.

die Federung.
Mit dem serienmäßigen, porsche-sperrsynchronisierten Fünfgang-Getriebe läßt sich der 911 SC immer im optimalen Drehzahlbereich bewegen. Das Getriebegehäuse besteht, um Gewicht einzusparen, aus dem sehr leichten Silumin. Das Differential ist identisch mit dem Ausgleichsgetriebe der Porsche-Spitzen-Modelle Turbo und 928; auf Wunsch wird es mit 40% Sperrwirkung geliefert.
Der Antrieb der Hinterräder erfolgt über Doppelgelenkwellen. Eine verdrehweiche Kupplung mit serienmäßiger Kupplungshilfe erfordert nur wenig Pedaldruck und

bewirkt einen sehr komfortablen Kraftschluß beim Kuppeln.
Alle diese Fakten zeigen deutlich: »Langzeit-Qualität« beschränkt sich bei Porsche nicht allein auf eine für sechs Jahre garantierte Sicherheit vor Durchrostungsschäden an tragenden Karosserieteilen. Tatsächlich steht viel mehr dahinter: eine konstruktive Überdimensionierung aller Baugruppen in der Werkstoffwahl, in der Belastbarkeit und im geringen Anspruch an Wartung und Pflege.
Diese Eigenschaften sichern und erhalten den optischen und technischen Neuwert jedes Porsche auf viele Jahre und machen ge-

brauchte Porsche-Wagen zu ebenso begehrenswerten wie risikolosen Kaufobjekten.

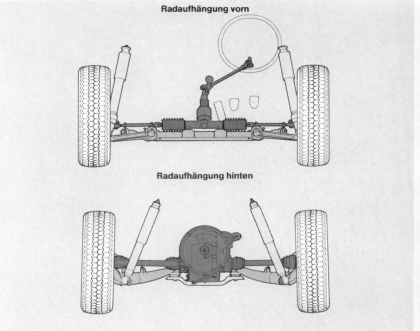

Radaufhängung vorn

Radaufhängung hinten

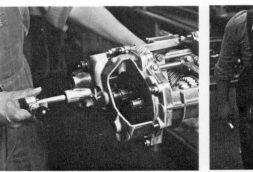

At the end of the seventies, there were only two versions of the motor, namely the 911 SC and the turbo, now also called 911, which gained even more performance as of 1978, achieving an easy 300 horsepower from 3.3-liter displacement.

911 TURBO charging principles

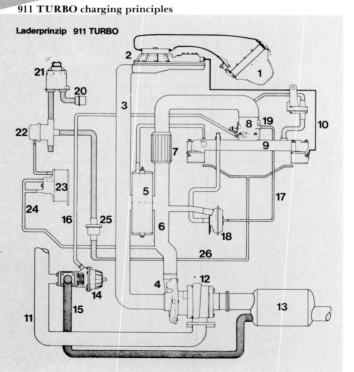

Laderprinzip 911 TURBO

Laderprinzip TURBO

1 Luftfilter
2 Gemischregler
3 Saugleitung
4 Turbolader (Verdichter)
5 Abblaseventil
6 Druckleitung
7 Ladeluftkühler
8 Drosselklappengehäuse
9 Luftverteiler
10 Kraftstoffeinspritzung
11 Abgas-Sammelleitung
12 Turbolader (Turbine)
13 Abgasschalldämpfer
14 Ladedruckregelventil
15 Bypassleitung
16 Steuerleitungen
17 Umluftsteuerleitung
18 Umluftventil
19 Ladeüberdruck-Sicherheitsschalter
20 Luftfilter
21 Zusatzluftpumpe
22 Abblaseumschaltventil
23 Steuerventil
24 Steuerleitung
25 Rückschlagventil
26 Lufteinblaseleitung

TURBO charging principles

1. Air filter
2. Mixing regulator
3. Intake piping
4. Compressor
5. Blowoff valve
6. Compression piping
7. Air cooler
8. Throttle valve housing
9. Air divider
10. Fuel injection
11. Exhaust collector piping
12. Turbine
13. Muffler
14. Pressure regulating vent
15. Bypass piping
16. Control mechanism
17. Bypass mechanism
18. Bypass vent
19. High-pressure safety valve
20. Air filter
21. Auxiliary air pump
22. Blowoff shift vent
23. Control vent
24. Control mechanism
25. Blowback vent
26. Air intake piping

Compressed air	Ladeluft
Sucked-in air	Saugluft
Additional air	Zusatzluft
Control pressure	Steuerdruck
Exhaust bypass of the charger	Abgasumgehung des Laders
Exhaust to the charger	Abgase zum Lader

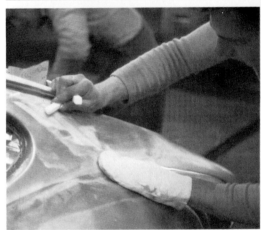

Sales brochures showed the careful preparation of the 911 types in great detail, and one must grant that this sports car is solid to an extraordinary degree.

Die Motoren.

The Motors
The six-cylinder Porsche power plants are compact, flat and weight-sparing boxer motors with three cylinders each in two opposed banks.

The Turbo 3.3 is easy to recognize by its widened fenders and its rubber-rimmed rear spoiler, but many drivers of other 911s also liked to decorate their cars with these sporting attributes.

This catalog of the reborn Carrera appeared in all its noble simplicity in 1984, showing the typically functional Porsche interior atmosphere without a snorkel.

Whoever knows how to get on with the 300-horsepower rear engine can experience the fun of driving in its fastest form, but it takes an experienced hand to control such great power safely.

EERING

he precise and
ntaneous steering action
e Porsche 911 is based on
proven principle of a safe
-and-pinion system.
racteristic of this
ciple are the simple and
 not vulnerable
struction, the optimal
ree of effect and the
llent contact between the
ring wheel and the

wheels. The pinion is
simultaneously a part of the
track rod. It functions over
the whole steering distance
every time, absolutely without
play. The steering system
thereby gives the driver
reliable information, for
example, when the car nears
the edge of the road or when
puddles, ice or dirt decrease
the friction between tires and
road.

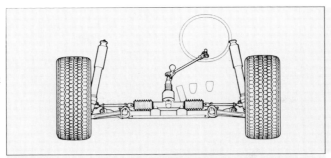

ignition spark,
s at the right
is provided by
1 Turbo's
ctless condensor
ion, and in the
Carrera models
DME (Digital
r Electronic)
ion system.

1. Fuel pump
2. Fuel filter
3. Pressure damper
3a. Pressure regulator
4. Injection piping
5. Idle control
6. Air gauge
7. Throttle valve switch
8. Air intake thermostat
9. Motor thermostat
10. RPM sensor
11. Code sensor
12. Control mechanism
13. Injection vent(s)
14. Coil
15. Distributor
16. Double relays: fuel pump control
17. Idle switch
18. Securing box

DME
Injection
System

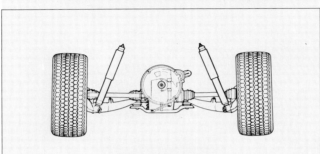

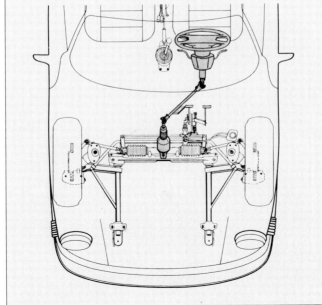

Fuel supply

Low pressure control

Transistor ignition

DIE LENKUNG.

Das präzise und spontane
Lenkverhalten des Porsche 911
basiert auf dem bewährten Prinzip einer Sicherheits-Zahnstan-
genlenkung. Charakteristisch für
dieses Prinzip sind die einfache
und deshalb störungsunanfällige
Bauart, der optimale Wirkungsgrad und der ausgezeichnete
Kontakt zwischen Lenkrad und
Rädern. Die Zahnstange stellt

gleichzeitig einen Teil der Spur-
stange dar. Sie arbeitet selbst-
nachstellend und bauartbedingt
jederzeit über den gesamten
Lenkbereich absolut ohne Spiel.
Das Lenksystem vermittelt dem
Fahrer daher zuverlässige Informationen, zum Beispiel wenn
sich der Wagen dem Grenzbe-
reich nähert oder wenn Pfützen,
Eisglätte oder Schmutz den
Reibwert zwischen Reifen und
Fahrbahn verringern.

**Den zündenden
Funken zum jeweils
richtigen Zeitpunkt
liefert im 911 Turbo
eine kontaktlose
Kondensatorzün-
dung und in den
neuen Carrera-
Modellen eine DME
(Digitale Motor-
Elektronik)-Zünd-
anlage.**

1 Kraftstoffpumpe
2 Kraftstoffilter
3 Druckdämpfer
3a Druckregler
4 Einspritzleitungen
5 Leerlaufdrehsteller
6 Luftmengenmesser
7 Drosselklappen-schalter
8 Ansauglufttemperaturfühler
9 Motortemperaturfühler

10 Drehzahlsensor
11 Bezugsmarken-sensor
12 Steuergerät
13 Einspritzventil(e)
14 Zündspule
15 Zündverteiler
16 Doppelrelais: Kraftstoffpumpe Steuergerät
17 Leerlaufschalter
18 Sicherungsdose

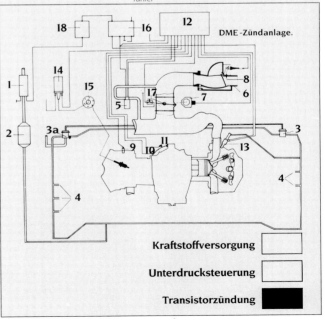

DME-Zündanlage.

Kraftstoffversorgung	
Unterdrucksteuerung	
Transistorzündung	■

Bei Dunkelheit kann sich der Porsche 911-Fahrer auf die Wirkung leuchtstarker H4-Halogenscheinwerfer verlassen.

Durch seine hohe Formfestigkeit und die konstruktiv bedingte selbsttätige Spannung sitzt das Verdeck immer richtig. Aufgrund seiner ausgeklügelten Mechanik und seines geringen Gewichts läßt es sich mit wenigen Handgriffen in kürzester Zeit öffnen und schließen.

In darkness the Porsche 911 driver can depend on the effect of strong H4 halogen headlights.

A useful criterion for good climate in the Porsche 911 is the steel sliding roof with automatically erecting wind deflector, available as optional equipment on the Carrera coupe.

Ein nützliches Kriterium für das gute Klima im Porsche 911 ist das als Sonderausstattung für das Carrera Coupé und den Turbo erhältliche Stahlschiebedach mit automatisch aufstellendem Windabweiser.

The folding roof of the Porsche 911 Carrera Targa can be taken off easily by hand, folded up and stowed in the luggage space.

Das Faltdach des Porsche 911 Carrera Targa ist mit wenigen Handgriffen abgenommen, zusammengeklappt und im Gepäckraum verstaut.

Because it holds its shape to a high degree and is constructed to maintain its tension, the cover always sits right. On the basis of its ingenious mechanics and light weight, it can be opened and closed by hand in the shortest time.

74

LOOK FORWARD TO AN INCOMPARABLE EXPERIENCE

Right: With the newest electronic methods the functioning of the Porsche aggregate can be checked in modern workshops, which makes exact installation of the complex components possible.

Left: In 1982 the long-desired full convertible joined the 911s, since the Targa never was fully accepted as one by most convertible fans.

As you could see and read on the preceding pages, the Porsche 911 is a typical product "in the style of the house," a perfect synthesis of attractive styling, sporting characteristics, progressive motor and suspension technology and a very high degree of construction and preparation quality. It provides reliability and everyday practicality, driving and service comfort, active and passive safety.

That this perfect synthesis of apparently contradictory characteristics is based on thorough understanding of research and development in almost every area of automobile construction and on purposeful participation in motor sports, you can learn from a further brochure that we will be happy to give you.

Naturally you also can get detailed information about all the other Porsche models—the Porsche 924, the 944 and 928 S—concerning their technology, safety features and equipment when you contact your Porsche dealer directly or request the appropriate catalog from us. Your dealer also can make possible an incomparable experience that will make known to you the whole fascination of Porsche driving, which you therefore should not pass up: a test drive in a Porsche. Look forward to it—we look forward to your reaction.

FREUEN SIE SICH AUF EIN UNVERGLEICHLICHES ERLEBNIS.

Wie Sie auf den vorhergehenden Seiten sehen und lesen konnten, ist der Porsche 911 ein typisches Produkt »nach Art des Hauses«: eine perfekte Synthese aus attraktivem Styling, sportlichen Fahreigenschaften, fortschrittlichen Motor- und Fahrwerkstechnologien und einem Höchstmaß an Konstruktions- und Fertigungsqualität, Zuverlässigkeit und Alltagstauglichkeit, Fahr- und Bedienungskomfort, aktiver und passiver Sicherheit.

Daß diese perfekte Synthese scheinbar widersprüchlicher Eigenschaften auf umfassenden Erkenntnissen aus der Forschung und Entwicklung in nahezu allen Teilbereichen des Automobilbaus und aus einem gezielten Engagement im Motorrennsport basiert, können Sie einer weiteren Broschüre entnehmen, die wir Ihnen ebenfalls gerne zur Verfügung stellen.

Selbstverständlich können Sie auch für alle anderen Porsche-Modelle – den Porsche 924, den Porsche 944 und den Porsche 928 S – detaillierte Informationen über die Technik, die Sicherheitsmerkmale und die Ausstattung erhalten, wenn Sie sich direkt mit ihrem Porsche-Händler in Verbindung setzen oder wenn Sie von uns den entsprechenden Modellkatalog anfordern. Ihr Händler kann Ihnen außerdem ein unvergleichliches Erlebnis ermöglichen, das Ihnen erst die ganze Faszination des Porsche-Fahrens vermittelt und das Sie sich schon deshalb in keinem Fall entgehen lassen sollten: die Probefahrt mit einem Porsche. Freuen Sie sich darauf – wir freuen uns auf Ihre Reaktion.

Der neue Porsche 911 Carrera.

Paßt ein Auto nach mehr als zwanzigjähriger Bauzeit noch in unsere Zeit? Diese Frage werden viele Fahrer eines Porsche 911 gerne beantworten. Sie werden mit Sicherheit von vielen unvergeßlichen Erlebnissen mit ihrem »Porsche 911« zu erzählen wissen, vom unvergeßlichen Spaß, den er bereitet.

Oder sie erzählen, wie sich der »911« im Laufe der Zeit den Anforderungen der Zeit durch den Einsatz neuer Technologien nicht nur immer wieder anzupassen verstand, sondern

Dazu gehört, daß der Motor mit digitaler Elektronik arbeitet, die sowohl die Einspritzung als auch die Zündung steuert. Das bedeutet: ein besonders verbrauchsarmes Start- und Kaltlaufverhalten, Abschaltung der Kraftstoffzufuhr im Schiebebetrieb, eine optimale Gemischanreicherung im Vollastbetrieb und eine Steigerung des Motorwirkungsgrads durch die auf die jeweiligen Betriebsbedingungen exakt angepaßten Zündwinkel. Das Drehmoment des Motors wuchs noch, er ist drehfreudiger und elastischer geworden.

ihnen oft sogar voraus war. Was letzten Endes das sicherste Anzeichen dafür ist, wie fortschrittlich die Konzeption des Klassikers unter den Porsche-Modellen von Anfang an war.

Die Prämisse für die Entwicklung des Porsche 911 Carrera hieß zum Beispiel: mehr Leistung bei gleichzeitig weniger Verbrauch. Daß der neue Carrera diese auf den ersten Blick widersprüchlichen Anforderungen erfüllen kann, ist einer ganzen Reihe von technischen Verbesserungen zu verdanken, die weit über das übliche Maß von Modellpflegemaßnahmen hinausgehen.

Der luftgekühlte Sechszylinder-Boxermotor aller neuen Carrera-Modelle (Coupé, Targa und Cabriolet) leistet – mit einem Hubraum von 3,2 l und dem hohen Verdichtungsverhältnis von 10,3 : 1 |9,5 : 1| – 170 kW (231 PS) |152 kW (207 PS)| bei 5.900 Umdrehungen/min. Das Maximum des Drehmomentverlaufs liegt mit 284 Nm |262 Nm| bei 4.800 Umdrehungen/min. Die durch Kraftstoffunterbrechung begrenzte Höchstdrehzahl beträgt ca. 6.500 Umdrehungen/min.

| | Katalysator-Werte

The new Porsche 911 Carrera

Is a car still suited to our time after being built for more than twenty years? Many drivers of the Porsche 911 will be happy to answer this question. They will be able to tell of many unforgettable experiences with a Porsche 911, of the unforgettable joy that it provides.

Or they'll tell how during the course of time the 911 not only always knew how to meet the demands of the time through the use of new technology, but often was ahead of its time. In the end, this is the surest sign of how advanced the conception of the classic among Porsche models was from the start.

The premise for the development of the Porsche 911 Carrera, for example, called for more performance and less consumption at the same time. That the new Carrera can fulfill these obviously contradictory demands is the result of a whole series of technical improvements that go far beyond the usual run of model development.

Then too, the motor runs with digital electronics that control both the fuel injection and the ignition. That makes for particularly thrifty starting and cold running, switching off the fuel induction when shifting, an optimal enriching of the mixture under a full load and a heightening of the degree of motor functioning by the ignition angles. The motor's torque has increased to become more powerful and elastic.

The air-cooled six-cylinder boxer motor in all new Carrera models (coupe, Targa and convertible) produces—with a displacement of 3.2 liters and the high compression ratio of 10.3 : 1—170 kW (231 hp) at 5900 revolutions per minute. The maximum torque production of 284 Nm (262 Nm) takes place at 4800 revolutions per minute. The highest engine speed, limited by fuel interruption, amounts to 6500 revolutions per minute.

(catalisator values)

Thanks to more than twenty years of experience in developing the 911, the Carrera, back in the catalog as of 1984, is a 231-horsepower sports car whose total quality scarcely can be exceeded.

When the 911 convertible went into production, a dream came true for many Porsche drivers; a ride in such a potent open car in nice weather is a high point in driving pleasure.

The Porsche model program

uch successful cars as the Porsche , Carrera RSR Turbo and the /936 series (which to this day are most successful racing cars of all e) emphasize the experience of rsche constructors in the area of bocharging—experience that was sequently applied to the Porsche Turbo. In the same way perience in the everyday use of the rbo was used for new world ampion Turbos: the 956, 962 and TAG Turbo of the McLaren m in Formula 1. Who knows, haps the great victories of Laren drivers Niki Lauda and ain Prost would not have opened if the Porsche 911 Turbo not existed.

What always has been the premise Porsche competition cars also ounts to the best guarantee for everyday usefulness of the rsche 911 Turbo: the reliability, quality and the safety. What is portant for the racing Porsches's lap times also brings pleasure to 911 Turbo driver with the hest safety reserves, the high eleration performance, the aracteristic roadholding and nering.

The air-cooled six-cylinder motor with exhaust turbocharger, with a displacement of 3.3 liters and a compression ratio of 7.0 : 1, produces 221 kW (300 hp) at 5500 revolutions per minute. The maximum torque is 430 Nm at 4000 revolutions per minute. The highest turning speed, limited by the ignition switching, is approximately 7000 revolutions per minute.

This power plant helps the 911 Turbo to achieve impressive performance: from 0 to 62 mph in 5.4 seconds; top speed of 162 mph. The fuel consumption (according to EWG Norm 80/1268) is 2.5 gallons at a steady 56 mph, 3 gallons at a steady 75 mph, and for the EG exhaust city-cycle 4 gallons per 62 miles.

What is important for the racing Porsche's fast lap times also means driving pleasure and safety reserves for the 911 Turbo driver.

So erfolgreiche Fahrzeuge wie der Porsche 917, der Carrera RSR Turbo und die Reihe der 935/936 (die bis heute als erfolgreichste Rennwagen aller Zeiten gelten), verdeutlichen die Erfahrungen der Porsche-Konstrukteure auf dem Gebiet der Turboaufladung. Erfahrungen, die im Porsche 911 Turbo konsequent umgesetzt wurden. Und genauso wurden die Erkenntnisse aus dem Alltagsbetrieb des Turbo wiederum für neue Weltmeister-Turbos genutzt: den 956, den 962 und – auch für den TAG-Turbo des McLaren-Teams in der

Was für die Wettbewerbsfahrzeuge von Porsche seit jeher die Voraussetzung für großartige Erfolge ist, bedeutet für den Porsche 911 Turbo gleichzeitig die beste Garantie für seine Alltagstauglichkeit: die Zuverlässigkeit, die Qualität und die Sicherheit. Und was für die Renn-Porsche wichtig ist für schnelle Rundenzeiten, bringt auch dem 911 Turbo-Fahrer Fahrvergnügen und höchste Sicherheitsreserven: die überlegenen Fahrleistungen, die hohen Querbeschleuni-

Was für die Renn-Porsche wichtig ist für schnelle Rundenzeiten, bedeutet für den 911 Turbo-Fahrer auch Fahrvergnügen und höchste Sicherheitsreserven.

Der luftgekühlte Sechszylinder-Motor mit Abgas-Turbolader leistet mit einem Hubraum von 3,3 l und einem Verdichtungsverhältnis von 7,0:1 221 kW (300 PS) bei 5.500 Umdrehungen/min. Das Maximum des Drehmomentverlaufs liegt mit 430 Nm bei 4.000 Umdrehungen/min. Die durch eine Zündabschaltung begrenzte Höchstdrehzahl beträgt ca. 7.000 Umdrehungen/min.

Dieses Triebwerk verhilft dem 911 Turbo zu beeindruckenden Fahrleistungen: von 0 auf 100 km/h in 5,4 s, Höchstgeschwindigkeit 260 km/h. Die Verbrauchswerte (nach EWG-Norm 80/1268): bei konstant 90 km/h 9,7 l, bei konstant 120 km/h 11,8 l und für den EG-Abgas-Stadtzyklus 15,5 l pro 100 km.

Formel 1. Wer weiß, vielleicht hätte es die großen Siege der McLaren-Piloten Niki Lauda und Alain Prost nicht gegeben, wenn es den Porsche 911 Turbo nicht gäbe?

gungswerte, das charakteristische Fahr- und Kurvenverhalten.

The Porsche 911 as Seen in the Press

After the new Porsche sports car that was to replace the venerable 356 was presented at the 1963 Frankfurt Auto Show, it still took until the fall of the following year before production started. The auto magazine *Auto, Motor and Sport (AMS)* already had been granted the privilege in August of 1964 of being the first specialist journal in the world to test a pre-production 901. Before one got down to the individual details of the brand new car, one could first let the body styling have its effect. "The basic form of the body was retained, and that may well be why the 901 is identified by the layman at first glance as a genuine Porsche. The body style may be accepted as tangible proof that creative talent has not died out in the third Porsche generation."

It was obvious that a great gamble had succeeded with the shape of the new Porsche. "The job of building a genuine Porsche that is likewise a modern automobile in terms of form hardly could have been solved more convincingly. There is no trace of mannerism to be seen in the whole car, no grasping at short-lived effects."

But it was not just the outer skin that pleased at once; the interior and the available luggage space also were far better than in the old 356. When one sat down, one enjoyed the best view. "The graceful exterior is not just a matter of taste, but also provides a much better view than one was accustomed to in the old 356. The deep beltline and the higher windows lack nothing of the progress that coach-building has made in this respect. That also is true of the view to the rear: the slight tilt was balanced out by the large area of the rear window; the view through it is sufficiently distortion-free." But now to assess that which truly characterizes this sports car—that was the new six-cylinder motor. "From outside one hears that 'Porrsch' that always inspires enthusiasm, especially in southern lands, even though, as a conglomerate of exhaust and mechanical sounds, it stimulates the auditory organs responsible for type-testing. The arrangement of the exhaust pipe is not yet final."

After this first experience, so typical of Porsches, the motor had to show in use whether it could fulfill the high expectations that it was meant to meet. But the tester soon was convinced of the power plant's quality. "Our concern as to whether this first six-cylinder motor from the house of Porsche, the fourth motor built by Porsche since the war, is as inspiring as its predecessors (all of which still are being built!) was without basis. After a few kilometers we were convinced by this machine, not only because of its sound, and not only because it runs so flexibly that one can drive at 37 mph in fifth gear, but also because of its extraordinary ability to turn and its absolutely trustworthy performance at high speed."

With its eight crankshaft bearings and a very undersquare relationship between bore and stroke, the motor was built to be run at high speeds without fear for its longevity. The shift pattern of the otherwise very smoothly functioning five-speed gearbox was unusual. "First gear is not meant to be used at times to spare the engine, but is a normal driving gear. It is found in the shift pattern at the place where one is accustomed to find fourth gear; correspondingly, fourth gear is in the place of third, third in place of second and second in place of first in the normal shift pattern. To engage first gear, one

Porsche 911 2 liter, prepared to compete in the 1965 Monte Carlo Rally. At that time rally cars were still basically stock.

must push the lever to the left and then pull it toward oneself."

In this gearbox the fifth gear was not meant to spare the engine either, but took the place of the otherwise direct fourth gear. The sporting driver thus always had the option of choosing the optimal gear to utilize the performance of the 130-hp motor.

On the other hand, the 901 was not planned as an uncompromising sports car. The choice of the comfortable suspension also was made very carefully. "The suspension comfort is astounding for a car with such a short wheelbase; even long waves in the surface are handled without sudden vertical movements or jerks of the car. The car clearly is more softly sprung than the Carrera and the 356 C and SC models (which have been softened). A final solution still is being worked out, including a way to reduce the still-existing tendency to lean to the side."

Seen as a whole, the pre-production test car made a very positive and promising impression on the tester.

"No question about it, the new sports car that will be produced in Zuffenhausen as of the end of August is one of the most interesting cars in the world."

Two years later the legendary 160-hp 911 S appeared, and *AMS* again obtained a test car. The motor stood out not only for its power, but also for its remarkable flexibility. "The motor runs so elastically that one can drop to about 1000 rpm when speed is not wanted. Thus it is quite possible to use fifth gear in normal traffic, even in the city, as it can be used over a wide range of speed from about 30 to about 143 mph."

When its performance was being measured, the test car accelerated from zero to 62 mph in only 7.6 seconds and reached a top speed of 138 mph. Fortunately this car's brakes also proved to be fully sufficient. "After three weeks of driving, even on demanding steep roads in the mountains, we can give the brakes the highest grade. For all-out racing purposes their performance potential certainly can be increased through harder setting—which demands harder foot power—but for street use the presently chosen compromise is undoubtedly right."

In the steering a compromise had been reached that allowed precise steering but also caused a disadvantage. "There scarcely can be a car in which road surface influences make themselves felt so strongly in the steering. When changing the car's position—especially in reverse—one must be very careful that an uneven spot in the surface or a curbstone does not tear the wheel out of one's hand. When driving on rough roads it is necessary to absorb and compensate for the effects of bumps lightly with one's arms—all things that are scarcely necessary in other steering systems." But as a whole the 911 S was rated very highly, as expected. One really could sense the tester's pleasure in this purebred sports car. In May of 1967 the same magazine tested the still-very-new Targa version of the 911 S. The test began with the tester trying desperately to help two Porsche lady drivers who were surprised by rain close the Targa roof, which was done only after a lot of trouble. But then the advantages of the Targa are discussed. "The front and back parts of the roof can be opened separately. Thus one can look out the back without having the front open and look out the front without having the back open. But one also can look out both ways, or have both closed."

The whole report is written in a very humorous style, and reading it gives one a real "appetite" for this car. Since the car has the S-car's motor, it has a particular charm in that the performance of the Targa is no less than that of the coupe. "I admit: It always impresses me to see how the motor always takes off over 3000 rpm and continues to over 7000 rpm, and how even on curves and on wet or bumpy roads, the car reacts to the gas pedal—without swinging, without breaking loose. It is a very great pleasure."

In 1969 the displacement of all 911s was increased to 2.2 liters by enlarging the bore, which gave *AMS* a new reason to put the sports car to the test. The new motors offered the greatest changes and advances. "The most advantageous changes have been in the performance and turning moment curves of the three 911 cars of types T, E and S. They run more smoothly and richly and attain higher top results at lower engine speeds." The T and E versions were tested with 125 and 155 hp respectively, which compared to their predecessors, each with 51 horsepower less, had not become much faster but showed marked improvement in flexibility and noise reduction. As for borderline performance, the Porsche could be surprising now as before.

"The fact has not changed that one must handle this fast car at the borderline with sensitivity and caution to be sure of avoiding surprises. The car reacts especially unpleasantly, for example, when one backs off the gas on a sharp curve, when shifting or, quite naturally, braking."

Good quality, on the other hand, was found in the area of workmanship. "The other revisions to the Porsche 911 were intended to make the car's standard of quality live up to its high price range. A lot of invisible small-scale work was done, especially to the bodywork, because the first series had a long list of complaints. In the 911 C one definitely has the impression of sitting in a quality car: the workmanship is faultless in every detail, and only high-value materials are used." The magazine *Motor-Rundschau* tested the then-least-powerful 911 in 1970, the 125-hp T model. These testers too could say nothing negative about the machine. "Actually this motor pleased us very well. It is very elastic and very smooth. But there, where a sedan's motor usually comes to the end of its performance, the T motor keeps going actively."

Yet they had serious criticism to offer as well in reference to the sometimes tricky handling. "But a good motor alone does not make a good car. And as much as the motor pleased us, we still regret just as much that a part of the handling characteristics under the high demands that one can and must place on such an expensive car is not satisfactory."

Driving a Porsche at high speed required, then as before, an experienced driver, but otherwise the car did not demand any unusual treatment. "Starting out with a warm or cold motor is no problem; it

Porsche 911 S 2.2 liter. This car took part in the 1971 East African Safari Rally.

always reacts cleanly to the commands of the gas pedal. Nor are starting and running disturbed by constant short-distance or city driving."

In 1974 *AMS* tested a very different Porsche: the Carrera RS. This light-bodied coupe weighed only 2332 pounds, but at 230 hp it was then the most powerful production car in Germany. It cost almost 65,000 Marks but offered exclusive technology. "Under the gigantic fenders are eight- or nine-inch rims, which are mounted with 60 tires, giving the dimensions of 215/15 (front) and 235/15 (rear) and necessarily conceal what moves the final price of the lightweight car into the realm of dream cars: the disc brakes of the 917 Turbo. They alone cost as much as a good-sized middle-class car, and they make clear even more than the motor how thoroughly the technicians of the house have devoted themselves to the Carrera project."

Truly breathtaking performance thus could be achieved with such a sports car. "There is no doubt that this is a case of high performance in the truest sense of the word once one pushes the accelerator all the way down. For the way this potent sprinter sets itself in motion seeks its equal—to be sure, without a real chance of finding anything similar. Most impressive, certainly, is the ability to accelerate in the two lowest gears, which when needed react so instantly that one has trouble keeping up with changing gears. Sixty-two mph is reached in barely over five seconds, and even 80 is reached in one short breath. The reason for this almost painful transition into the fastest speeds, which also provides a clear superiority to the usually sovereign phalanz of Italian super-sports cars, is not based only on the favorable weight and handling, but even more on the very special way a Porsche puts its power on the road.

Practically nothing is lost, at least on a dry road—the resulting push has something of what results when one needs no wheels to get moving, but rather a towline or a jet thrust."

"Above 112 mph the air resistance sets unexpectedly clear limits to the powerful forward motion of the Carrera RS. The braking system, that even could handle the 12000 horsepower of the 917, and the roadholding that is clearly better than that of the other 911s, allow fascinating action with this car. There was no cause for worry about finding customers for the 100 examples required for sanction."

Just a year later this magazine was able to test a different dream car—the Porsche Turbo—which still is available today in similar form. The firm wanted to use this top-of-the-line model to break into the international upper class, which then consisted of Italian and English exotic cars, and as we know today, this purpose was achieved impressively.

Above: 911 S 2.5 liter, a competitor in the 1972 Monte Carlo Rally.

Left: Another relative of the Porsche 911: the Type 934 Turbo RSR, a Group 4 racing sports car as of 1976.

For many years an excellent periodical for all Porsche fans has been in print. Founded by Richard von Frankenberg and edited today by Reinhard Seiffert, it now as then is a publication of very high quality. For 36 Marks per year one can subscribe to the quarterly magazine, called *Christophorus*. The address: P.O. Box 40 06 40, 7000 Stuttgart 40. West Germany.

At upper left a 911 **RSR** 2.8 liter at **Le Mans** in 1973; at left a 300-horsepower 1984 Turbo 3.3 liter.

Lower left: The 1977 models, with the 924 in the background. At right, the 911 C convertible, presented in March of 1982.

Interior of a 1977
Porsche 911 with the
new central console.

indeed, but naturally the turbo motor was the most important element of the car.

"It is not sheer acceleration alone, though, that fascinates, but even more the way it is provided. Like a jet engine, the turbo motor provides a fully new dimension in power transfer, which is essentially a result of its wide usable power curve. It especially is impressive that all this takes place remarkably quietly and unbelievably gently."

In the Turbo too, borderline handling could be handled only by experienced drivers, and the tester would have liked better ventilation of the front brakes. Naturally, certain allowances had to be made in terms of riding comfort.

"That the Turbo is the most comfortable Porsche in terms of furnishings and road-noise damping already has been said. This admittedly is not true of the suspension comfort, which clearly is worse than in the other models on account of the stiff springs and shock absorbers. Yet the suspension is not at all unpleasant in its total impression."

Deeply impressed, the testers said farewell to this sports car, which ranks now as before among the most exciting cars in the world. "Without a doubt, Porsche has set new standards in cultivation and performance with the Turbo, and the technical achievement that the Turbo incorporates speaks not only for Porsche, but for German automobile construction and for performance cars as a whole."

"Undoubtedly Porsche has achieved its intended goal with the Turbo. The roller-like tires, the oversize fenders, the production front spoiler, but especially the sweeping rear wing assure it an unusual degree of attention. On the body itself there is not a gram of chrome to be found; even the side mirrors and headlight rings are a functional black."

Many luxurious details such as a headlight cleaning system, electric window controls and even a stereo radio and automatic heat regulation make traveling with this super-sports car very comfortable

Model	901	911/911 L	911 S	911 T
Year	1963	1964-1967	1966-1967	1967-1968
Body	Coupe	Coupe/Targa since 1966	Coupe/Targa	Coupe/Targa
Cylinders	6	6	6	6
Bore/Stroke	80 x 66	80 x 66	80 x 66	80 x 66
Displacement	1991 cc	1991 cc	1991 cc	1991 cc
Horsepower	130	130	160	110
At rpm	6200	6100	6600	5800
Torque/rpm	16.5/4600	17.8/4200	18.2/5200	16.0/4200
Compression	9:1	9:1	9.8:1	8.6:1
Wheelbase	2204 mm	2211 mm	2211 mm	2211 mm, 2268 mm in 1968
Front track	1332 mm	1337 mm, 1353 mm in 1966	1367 mm	1353 mm, 1367 mm in 1968
Rear track	1312 mm	1317 mm, 1325 mm in 1966	1339 mm, 1335 mm in 1967	1325 mm, 1335 mm in 1968
Tires	165 HR 15	165 HR 15	165 HR 15	165 HR 15
Length	4135 mm	4163 mm	4163 mm	4163 mm
Dry weight	2200 lbs.	2376 lbs., 2266 lbs. in 1966	2266 lbs., 2376 lbs. in 1967	2376 lbs., 2244 lbs. in 1968
Production	pre-prod.	Coupe 16,213, Targa 6120	Coupe 1790, Targa 1160	Coupe 5515, Targa 803
Original price in DM	DM 23,700	Coupe 21,000, Targa 22,400	Coupe 24,480, Targa 26,000	Coupe 19,000, Targa 20,400
0 to 62 mph	8.7 sec.	8.7 sec.	7.6 sec.	10 sec.
Top speed	130 mph	130 mph	137 mph	137 mph

Model	911 E	911 S	911 T 2.2	911 E 2.2
Year	1968	1968	1969-1971	1969-1971
Body	Coupe/Targa	Coupe/Targa	Coupe/Targa	Coupe/Targa
Cylinders	6	6	6	6
Bore/stroke	80 x 66	80 x 66	84 x 66	84 x 66
Displacement	1991 cc	1991 cc	2195 cc	2195 cc
Horsepower	140	170	125	155
At rpm	6500	6800	5800	6200
Torque/rpm	17.8/4500	18.5/5500	18/4200	19.5/4500
Compression	9.1:1	9.9:1	8.6:1	9.1:1
Wheelbase	2268 mm	2268 mm	2268 mm	2268 mm
Front track	1374 mm, Targa 1364 mm	1374 mm	1374 mm	1374 mm
Rear track	1355 mm, Targa 1345 mm	1355 mm	1343 mm	1355 mm
Tires	185/70VR15	185/70VR15	185/70VR15	185/70VR15
Length	4163 mm	4163 mm	4163 mm	4163 mm
Dry weight	2244 lbs.	2101 lbs.	2398 lbs.	2442 lbs.
Production	Coupe 1968, Targa 858	Coupe 1492, Targa 614		
Original price in DM	Coupe 24,700 Targa 26,480	Coupe 26,920 Targa 28,700	Coupe 19,969 Targa 23,199	Coupe 24,975 Targa 26,925
0 to 62 mph	9 sec.	8 sec.	9.4 sec.	9 sec.
Top speed	134 mph	140 mph	130 mph	134 mph

Model	911 S 2.2	911 T 2.4	911 E 2.4	911 S 2.4
Year	1969-1971	1971-1973	1971-1973	1971-1973
Body	Coupe/Targa	Coupe/Targa	Coupe/Targa	Coupe/Targa
Cylinders	6	6	6	6
Bore/Stroke	84 x 66	84 x 70.4	84 x 70.4	84 x 70.4
Displacement	2195 cc	2341 cc	2341 cc	2341 cc
Horsepower	180	130	165	190
At rpm	6500	5600	6200	6500
Torque/rpm	20.3/5200	20/4000	21/4500	22/5200
Compression	9.8:1	7.5:1	8:1	8.5:1
Wheelbase	2268 mm	2271 mm	2271 mm	2271 mm
Front track	1374 mm	1360 mm	1372 mm	1372 mm
Rear track	1355 mm	1342 mm	1354 mm	1354 mm
Tires	185/70VR15	165 HR 15	185/70VR15	185/70VR15
Length	4080 mm	4147 mm	4147 mm	4147 mm
Dry weight	2046 lbs.	2442 lbs.	2442 lbs.	2442 lbs.
Production				
Original price in DM	Coupe 27,140 Targa 29,090	Coupe 22,980 Targa 25,200	Coupe 25,980 Targa 28,200	Coupe 30,680 Targa 32,900
0 to 62 mph	7.4 sec.	9.5 sec.	8.5 sec.	7.5 sec.
Top speed	142 mph	127 mph	137 mph	143 mph

Model	Carrera RS 2.7	911 2.7	911 S 2.7	Carrera 3.0
Year	1972-1975	1973-1976	1973-1976	1975-1978
Body	Coupe	Coupe/Targa	Coupe/Targa	Coupe/Targa
Cylinders	6	6	6	6
Bore/Stroke	90 x 84	90 x 70.4	90 x 70.4	95 x 70.4
Displacement	2687 cc	2687 cc	2687 cc	2993 cc
Horsepower	210	150	175	200
At rpm	6300	5700	5800	6000
Torque/rpm	26/5100	24/3800	24/4000	26/4200
Compression	8.5:1	8:1	8.5:1	8.5:1
Wheelbase	2271 mm	2271 mm	2271 mm	2271 mm
Front track	1372 mm	1360 mm	1372 mm	1372 mm
Rear track	1380 mm	1342 mm	1380 mm	1380 mm
Tires	185/70VR15	165 HR 15	185/70VR15	185/70VR15
Rear tires	215/60VR15	same	same	215/60VR15
Length	4291 mm	4291 mm	4291 mm	4291 mm
Dry weight	2442 lbs./RS 2200 lbs.	2365 lbs.	2365 lbs.	2464 lbs.
Production				
Original price in DM	Coupe 35500 Targa 37720	Coupe 2700 Targa 29000	Coupe 31000 Targa 33000	Coupe 44950 Targa 47450
0 to 62 mph	6.5 sec.	8.5 sec.	7.6 sec.	6.3 sec.
Top speed	149 mph	130 mph	140 mph	146 mph

Model	930 Turbo	911	911 SC	930 Turbo 3.3
Year	1975-1978	1976-1978	1978-1980	1978-
Body	Coupe	Coupe/Targa	Coupe/Targa	Coupe/Cvt.
Cylinders	6	6	6	6
Bore/Stroke	95 x 70.4	90 x 70.4	95 x 70.4	97 x 74.4
Displacement	2993 cc	2687 cc	2993 cc	3299 cc
Horsepower	260	165	180	300
At rpm	5500	5800	5500	5500
Torque/rpm	35/4000	24/4000	27/4200	43.8/4000
Compression	6.5:1	8.5:1	8.5:1	7:1
Wheelbase	2272 mm	2271 mm	2272 mm	2272 mm
Front track	1432 mm	1372 mm	1369 mm	1432 mm
Rear track	1502 mm	1354 mm	1379 mm	1501 mm
Frt. tires	205/50 VR15	185/70 VR15	185/70 VR15	205/55 VR16
Rear tires	225/50 VR15		215/60 VR15	225/50 VR16
Length	4291 mm	4291 mm	4291 mm	4291 mm
Dry weight	2640 lbs.	2464 lbs.	2552 lbs.	2937 lbs.
Production				see 911 SC
Original price in DM	65,800	Coupe 34,350, Targa 36,850		79,900
0 to 62 mph	5.6 sec.	7.5 sec	7 sec.	5.4 sec.
Top speed	155 mph	134 mph	140 mph	162 mph

Model	911 SC	911 SC	911 Carrera	911 Carrera Kat.
Year	1980-1981	1981-1985	1984-	1985-
Body	Coupe/Targa	Coupe/Targa	Coupe/Targa/Cvt.	Coupe/Targa/Cvt.
Cylinders	6	6	6	6
Bore/Stroke	95 x 70.4	95 x 70.4	95 x 74.4	95 x 74.4
Displacement	2956 cc	2956 cc	3164 cc	3164 cc
Horsepower	188	204	231	207
At rpm	5500	5900	5900	5900
Torque/rpm	27/4200	24/4300	29/4800	27/4300
Compression	8.6:1	9.8:1	10.3:1	9.5:1
Wheelbase	2272 mm	2272 mm	2272 mm	2272 mm
Front track	1369 mm	1369 mm	1372 mm	1372 mm
Rear track	1379 mm	1379 mm	1380 mm	1380 mm
Front tires	185/70VR15	185/70VR15	185/70VR15	185/70VR16
Rear tires	215/60VR15	215/60VR15	215/60VR15	215/60VR15
Length	4291 mm	4291 mm	4291 mm	4291 mm
Dry weight	2552 lbs.	2552 lbs.	2772 lbs.	2772 lbs.
Production	Total production including 1985: Targa 66-85: 72,391, Coupe 64-85: 126,565, Convertible 82-85: 10,994, Turbo 74-85: 12,265			
0 to 62 mph	7 sec.	6.8 sec.	6.1 sec.	6.5 sec.
Top speed	140 mph	146 mph	152 mph	146 mph

Porsche 911 in Miniature

Seldom has such a variety of models been available to fill the miniature collector's showcase as in the case of Porsche. The models listed here are by no means all that have existed. Further variants also are on the market, including publicity gifts. The fact that the Porsche 911 is an evergreen is documented in this realm too! The very small scales, though, are not well represented.

Porsche 911 Coupe

Wiking (D)	Readymade	Plastic	1/160	
Playart (HK)	Readymade	Diecast	1/90	
Wiking (D)	Readymade	Plastic	1/87	
DBGM (D)	Readymade	Plastic	1/77	
Tootsietoys (USA)	Readymade	Diecast	1/75	
Schuco (D)	Readymade	Diecast	1/66	
Faller (D)	Readymade	Plastic	1/60	
Faller (D)	Readymade	Plastic	1/60	Rally
Siku (D)	Readymade	Diecast	1/60	
Siku (D)	Readymade	Diecast	1/60	Police
Siku (D)	Readymade	Diecast	1/60	Turbo
Siku (D)	Readymade	Diecast	1/60	Rally
Lintoy (HK)	Readymade	Tinplate	1/47	
Gama (D)	Readymade	Diecast	1/43	
Gama (D)	Readymade	Diecast	1/3	Police
Stanum Linea (F)	Readymade	Tinplate	1/43	1963
Stanum Linea (F)	Readymade	Tinplate	1/43	1981 Cvt.
Vitesse (P)	Readymade	Diecast	1/43	
Diapet (J)	Readymade	Diecast	1/42	
Diapet (J)	Readymade	Diecast	1/42	Police
Endoh (J)	Readymade	Tinplate	1/40	
K (J)	Readymade	Tinplate	1/36	Fire Chief
K (J)	Readymade	Tinplate	1/36	Police
CKO (D)	Readymade	Tinplate	1/35	
Fleischmann (D)	Readymade	Plastic	1/32	
Lucky (HK)	Readymade	Plastic	1/32	Police
Lucky (HK)	Readymade	Plastic	1/32	Fire Chief
Lucky (HK)	Readymade	Plastic	1/32	Rally
TT (J)	Readymade	Tinplate	1/32	
TT (J)	Readymade	Tinplate	1/32	Ambulance
TT (J)	Readymade	Tinplate	1/32	Fire Chief
TT (J)	Readymade	Tinplate	1/32	Police
Avon (USA)	Readymade	Glass	1/30	Perfume bottle
Carrera (D)	Readymade	Plastic	1/30	Slot racer

Plasto (SF)	Readymade	Plastic	1/28	
Heio (J)	Readymade	Tinplate	1/25	Police
Heio (J)	Readymade	Tinplate	1/25	Fire Chief
Revell (USA)	Kit	Plastic	1/25	
Fujimi (J)	Kit	Plastic	1/24	Turbo 1985
Fujimi (J)	Kit	Plastic	1/24	Carrera 1985
Fujimi (J)	Kit	Plastic	1/24	Carrera Cabrio 1985
Fujimi (J)	Kit	Plastic	1/24	Carrera 1973 Rally
Fujimi (J)	Kit	Plastic	1/24	R Coupe 1967
Guisval (E)	Readymade	Diecast	1/24	Rothmans
Guisval (E)	Readymade	Diecast	1/24	Martini
Guisval (E)	Readymade	Diecast	1/2/4	with skis
Martoys (I)	Readymade	Diecast	1/24	
Nacoral (E)	Readymade	Diecast	1/24	
Nacoral (E)	Readymade	Diecast	1/24	Rally
Mattel (USA)	Readymade	Diecast	1/22	Rally
Shinsei (J)	Readymade	Diecast	1/21	
TT (J)	Readymade	Tinplate	1/20	Sportomatic
Yone (J)	Readymade	Tinplate	1/19	
Yone (J)	Readymade	Tinplate	1/19	Police
Bandai (J)	Readymade	Plastic	1/16	
CB (J)	Readymade	Tinplate	1/16	
Daiya (J)	Readymade	Tinplate	1/16	
Taiyo (J)	Readymade	Tinplate	1/16	
Taiyo (J)	Readymade	Tinplate	1/16	Martini
Taiyo (J)	Readymade	Tinplate	1/16	Police
TPS (J)	Readymade	Tinplate	1/16	Rally
TPS (J)	Readymade	Tinplate	1/16	Patrol
TPS (J)	Readymade	Tinplate	1/16	Fire Chief

Porsche 911 S Coupe

Wiking (D)	Readymade	Plastic	1/87	SC
Wiking (D)	Readymade	Plastic	1/87	SC Cvt.
Best Box (NL)	Readymade	Diecast	1/66	
Efsi (NL)	Readymade	Diecast	1/66	
Efsi (NL)	Readymade	Diecast	1/66	Police

Efsi (NL)	Readymade	Diecast	1/66	Rally
Norev (F)	Readymade	Diecast	1/66	
Schuco (D)	Readymade	Diecast	1/66	
Schuco (D)	Readymade	Diecast	1/66	Police
Schuco (D)	Readymade	Diecast	1/66	Racing
Tomica (J)	Readymade	Diecast	1/61	
Tomica (J)	Readymade	Diecast	1/61	Police
Tomica (J)	Readymade	Diecast	1/61	Racing
Faller (D)	Readymade	Plastic	1/60	Police
AMR (F)	Kit	Metal	1/43	1963
Denzer (D)	Kit/R'made	Plastic	1/43	
Kirk (DK)	Readymade	Diecast	1/43	
Mebetoys (I)	Readymade	Diecast	1/43	
Mini Auto (GB)	Kit	Metal	1/43	
Metal 43 (F)	Kit	Metal	1/43	
RD Marmande (F)	Readymade	Wood	1/43	
SVC (F)	Kit/R'made	Plastic	1/43	
Tekno (DK)	Readymade	Diecast	1/43	
Vitesse (P)	Readymade	Diecast	1/43	
Vitesse (P)	Readymade	Diecast	1/42	Rally
Diapet (J)	Readymade	Diecast	1/41	
Jouef (F)	Readymade	Plastic	1/39	
Verve (I)	Readymade	Plastic	1/36	
Toy (HK) open	Readymade	Metal	1/36	SC Cvt.,
Toy (HK) closed	Readymade	Metal	1/36	SC Cvt,
Burago (I)	Readymade	Diecast	1/24	
Fujimi (J) 1973	Kit	Plastic	1/24	Carrera RS
Fujimi (J)	Kit	Plastic	1/24	Carrera RS 1974
Fujimi (J)	Kit	Plastic	1/24	1968
Martoys (I)	Readymade	Diecast	1/24	
Verve (I)	Readymade	Plastic	1/24	
Shinsei (J)	Readymade	Tinplate	1/2	
Daiya (J)	Readymade	Tinplate	1/16	
Daiya (J)	Readymade	Tinplate	1/16	Police
TPS (J)	Readymade	Tinplate	1/16	Racing
Woolco (J)	Readymade	Tinplate	1/16	

Porsche 911 Targa

Lindberg (USA)	Readymade	Plastic	1/60	
AMR (F)	Kit	Metal	1/43	1965
Corgi Toys (GB)	Readymade	Diecast	1/43	
Corgi Toys (GB)	Readymade	Diecast	1/43	Police
Denzer (D)	Kit/R'made	Plastic	1/43	
Eligor (F/CH)	Readymade	Diecast	1/43	1968
Eligor (F/CH)	Readymade	Diecast	1/43	1968 Rally
Eligor (F/CH)	Readymade	Diecast	1/43	1968 Police
Märklin (D)	Readymade	Diecast	1/43	
Minialuxe (F)	Readymade	Plastic	1/43	
Nacoral (E)	Readymade	Diecast	1/43	
Norev (F)	Readymade	Plastic	1/43	
RD Marmande (F)	Readymade	Wood	1/43	
Sablon (B)	Readymade	Diecast	1/43	
Sablon (B)	Readymade	Diecast	1/43	Police
Stelco (D)	Readymade	Vinyl	1/43	
Vinyl Line (D)	Readymade	Vinyl	1/43	
Vinyl Line (D)	Readymade	Vinyl	1/43	Police
Zwicky (CH)	Readymade	Plastic	1/43	
Strombecker (USA)	Kit	Plastic	1/39	
Märklin Sprint (D)	Readymade	Plastic	1/32	
Märklin Sprint (D)	Readymade	Plastic	1/32	Police
Huki (D)	Readymade	Tinplate	1/28	
Mebetoys (I)	Readymade	Diecast	1/25	
Fujimi (J)	Kit	Plastic	1/24	Carrera 1985
Lucky (HK)	Readymade	Plastic	1/21	Police
Lucky (HK)	Readymade	Plastic	1/21	Rally
Lucky (HK)	Readymade	Plastic	1/21	Police
Trico (HK)	Readymade	Plastic	1/21	Rally
Trico (HK)	Readymade	Plastic	1/20	
Wiron (D)	Readymade	Plastic	1/19	
Huki (D)	Readymade	Tinplate	1/19	
Huki (D)	Readymade	Tinplate	1/19	Rally
Huki (D)	Readymade	Tinplate	1/19	Police
Schuco (D)	Readymade	Plastic	1/16	
Nikko (J)	Readymade	Plastic	1/16	Rally
Nikko (J)	Readymade	Plastic	1/14	Police
MS (D)	Readymade	Plastic	1/14	
MS (D)	Readymade	Plastic	1/14	Police

Porsche Clubs

There are thousands of Porsche drivers all over the world and hundreds of organized Porsche clubs all over the world. There also are special 911 clubs. It is impossible to list them all here, and it would be unfair to list only some of them. For more specific information on this subject, write to the Publicity Department of the Dr. Ing. h. c. Porsche Co., Porschestrasse 42, 7000 Stuttgart 60, West Germany.

Books for the Porsche Fan

Das Grosse Porsche Buch, edited by Ingo Seiff. A 104-page color photo section on "Driving in its most beautiful form," including 40 pages of Weitmann photos. An illustrious team of authors from inside and outside Germany writes about the technical development and racing successes. 288 pages, clothbound, in slipcase.

Porsche—Geschichte und Technik der Renn- und Sportwagen, by Karl Ludvigsen. This Porsche bible in its German version ("Excellence was expected") is the most thorough chronological chronicle of the firm's history and catalog of Porsche models. It includes everything up to 1980. A precious book for all who love Porsches. 560 pages; more than 1000 illustrations, many in color.

Porsches for the Road, by Henry Rasmussen. This volume about Porsche cars appeared in the already-famous Survivor Series. It includes photo essays about the most important models, such as the 356A Speedster, 904 GTS, 911 2.7 Carrera and others. 250 illustrations, 125 in color; English.

Illustrated Porsche Buyer's Guide. All models are described with their technical data, specific strengths and weaknesses, and as investments and collectors' items. 176 pages, 200 black-and-white illustrations, English.

Das Grosse Buch der Porsche-Typen, by Lothar Boschen and Jürgen Barth. This second edition, expanded and brought up to date for 1980, is the great German-language standard work on the Porsche brand. It offers a complete typology of all vehicles, with all technical and historical data and a wealth of photo material. 716 pages, 833 photos and 29 drawings.

Porsche—The Complete Story, by Chris Harvey. In the Foulis Minimarque Series, this chronological overview covers the development of the Porsche brand from the 356 to the 928. 140 pages, English.

Porsche—Die Geschichte einer Denkfabrik, by Richard M. Langworth. Forty years of Porsche development are portrayed in this volume of pictures. Everything about the cars, their development, their changes and their various versions. 256 pages, 448 illustrations, 133 of them in color.

Porsche, by Chris Harvey. An interestingly organized and very advantageous volume of pictures in German about the Porsche brand. 64 pages, 83 color photos.

Porsche Museum, a documentation of the most important examples from the auto collection of the Porsche Museum.

Superb pictures make this volume a great pleasure. For every vehicle depicted you will find all the important technical data and historical details. An absolute must for every Porsche fan. 115 pages; 133 black-and-white and 110 color photos.

Porsche, in the Neko Historic Car Books, an opulent photo volume about all Porsche models. In 92 color and 62 black-and-white photos you even will find the new 944 Turbo and 959 models. 154 photos; Japanese.

Porsche—Great Marques Poster Book. This volume includes not only a short history of the firm but also the most important models of the brand, with all data and outstanding photos. The individual illustrations also can be framed. 48 pages, 24 color photos. English.

Porsche Past and Present, by Denis Jenkinson. The author, an English specialist in this brand, treats the firm and model history of the house of Porsche with great thoroughness, up to the Le Mans victory of 1982. 224 pages; 150 black-and-white photos. English.

Porsche Year 1982, by Susann C. Miller. The Porsche brand's and clubs' events of the season in America. 96 pages, more than 100 illustrations. English.

Porsche Year 1983-1984, by Susann Miller. Subsequent to the above. 96 pages, 125 black-and-white photos. English.

Porsche Year 1985-1986, by Susann Miller. The up-to-date sequel to the above. 96 pages, 94 black-and-white and 20 color photos. English.

Porsche—Carrera 6 to the 962, by Ian Bamsey. A complete and richly illustrated overview of all Porsche racing sports cars with detailed descriptions of the types. 192 pages, 48 color pages, 240 black-and-white photos. English.

The Porsche 911 Story, by Paul Frere. The author portrays all stages of development of this successful model by Porsche. Fully revised new edition. 304 pages, 191 illustrations, 7 pages in color.

The Porsche 911, by Chris Harvey. The developmental history with all technical information. Data and advice, comparison tests and much more. 256 pages, 200 illustrations, 16 pages in color. English.

Porsche 911 Turbo, by Michael Cotton. This volume in the "Auto Histories" series concerns the 3 and 3.3-liter models and

Project 930. 136 pages, 90 black-and-white photos and 8 pages in color. English.

Porsche 911 Carrera Superprofile, by Chris Harvey, treats the development of this series of models, gives much practical advice for restoring and repairing, and adds club information. 56 pages; 98 illustrations, 20 in color. English.

Porsche 911—A Collector's Guide, by Michael Cotton. This volume covers all Porsche 911 models and gives an overview of their developmental history as well as buying and repairing advice for older models. 128 pages, more than 140 illustrations. English.

Porsche 911/912—A Source Book. 144 pages, 300 illustrations. English.

Porsche 911: A Source Book. This volume covers 1974 to 1984. 144 pages, many black-and-white photos. English.

Porsche 911 Turbo—Grand Tourisme, by Michael Cotton. A volume in the French Grand Tourism Series, treating this model exhaustively. 130 pages, 90 black-and-white and 10 color photos. French.

Porsche—A History of Excellence. A richly illustrated volume about the house of Porsche with a complete type overview (including Volkswagen) from the first prototypes until today. 192 pages; 200 illustrations, some in color. English.

Porsche Story, by Julius Weitmann. Revised and expanded edition of this standard work on the Porsche brand. More than 600 photos. English.

Porsche, by Anders Ditlev Clausager. A combination of carefully researched firm and model history and excellent photo material. 224 pages; more than 300 illustrations, 150 in color. English.

The Classic Porsche, by Mike McCarthy. A photo volume in large format about the technical and historical development of the Porsche brand up to 1982. 98 pages, 100 color and 13 black-and-white photos. English.

Porsche 1980, a photo volume from Japan with excellent photo material; treats the 924 Turbo, 928, 911, 550A Spyder, 904 Carrera GTS, 356, 904, 1500 RS, 914. 196 illustrations, 91 in color. Japanese and English text.

Porsche Owner's Companion: A Manual of Preservation and Theft Protection, by Dan Werner Post. This book tells how Porsche owners can maintain the optimal values of their vehicles although using the cars regularly. 192 pages, 100 illustrations. English.

Porsche and Design, by Giancarlo Perini and Akira Fujimoto. This special volume 31½ of the Japanese publication *Car Styling* includes the complete development of the Porsche brand in terms of design and styling. 131 pages; many photos, many in color. Japanese and English.

Porsche Cars, by R. M. Clarke. These Brooklands publications include reprints of contemporary articles and road tests. 100 pages, English text. The following volumes exist at this time: *Porsche 911 1965-1969, Porsche 911 1970-1972, Porsche 911 1973-1977, Porsche Carrera 1973-1977, Porsche Turbo 1975-1984.*

Porsche Poster 1: Concours. An *Automobile Quarterly* collection poster with five photos of the following models: 924 Special 1977, 928 S 1982, 930 Turbo 1979, 944 1983, 911 SC convertible 1982. In color.

Porsche Poster 2: Concours. An *Automobile Quarterly* collection poster with five photos of the following models: 911 Carrera RS 3.0 1975, 911 S 1967, 911 Targa 1975, 911 1965, 914/6 1970. In color.

Porsche 911 Technical Poster. An *Automobile Quarterly* poster with one photo, one X-ray drawing and all technical data. In color.

Porsche 911 2.0, 2.2, 2.4, 2.7 L 63-75. Bucheli Repair Guide No. 324.

Porsche 911 (1970-1977). Autobooks Repair Guide No. 889. English.

Porsche 911 (1965-1985). Haynes Repair Guide No. 264. English.

Porsche 911 (E/S/SC/T) 1965-1982. A Clymer Repair Guide. 369 pages, 703 illustrations. English.

DEUTSCHMARK/DOLLAR CONVERSION CHART

YEAR	DEUTSCHMARKS PER DOLLAR
1954	4.1946
1956	4.2034
1958	4.1876
1960	4.2
1962	4.0
1964	3.9745
1966	4.0
1968	4.0
1970	3.6600
1972	3.2225
1974	2.5100
1976	2.5906
1978	2.0820
1980	1.7793
1982	2.3702
1984	2.7300
1986	2.3218
1988	1.7316
1989	1.8625

All figures note number of Deutschmarks equivalent to U.S. dollar at then-current exchange rates.